N. H Lee

Immersionists Against the Bible

The Babel builders confounded, in an exposition of the origin, design, tactics, and progress of the new version movement of Campbellites and other Baptists

N. H Lee

Immersionists Against the Bible

The Babel builders confounded, in an exposition of the origin, design, tactics, and progress of the new version movement of Campbellites and other Baptists

ISBN/EAN: 9783337100032

Printed in Europe, USA, Canada, Australia, Japan

Cover: Foto ©Lupo / pixelio.de

More available books at **www.hansebooks.com**

AGAINST

THE BIBLE;

OR,

THE BABEL BUILDERS CONFOUNDED,

IN AN EXPOSITION OF

THE ORIGIN, DESIGN, TACTICS, AND PROGRESS OF
THE NEW VERSION MOVEMENT OF CAMP-
BELLITES AND OTHER BAPTISTS.

BY THE

REV. N. H. LEE,

OF THE LOUISVILLE CONFERENCE.

EDITED BY THOMAS O. SUMMERS, D. D.

Contents.

PREFACE BY THE EDITOR.................................. iii

CHAPTER I.
INTRODUCTION 9

CHAPTER II.
THE ORIGIN OF THE MOVEMENT......................... 13

CHAPTER III.
THE MAIN DESIGN OF THE MOVEMENT 35

CHAPTER IV.
THE MAIN DESIGN, CONTINUED.......................... 54

CHAPTER V.
THE TACTICS OF THE MOVEMENT....................... 87

CHAPTER VI.
THE TACTICS OF THE MOVEMENT, CONTINUED......... 108

CHAPTER VII.
DISPARAGEMENT OF THE COMMON VERSION. 123

CHAPTER VIII.
THE IMMERSIONISTS HAVE DONE AND ARE DOING WHAT THEY CHARGE KING JAMES WITH DOING .. 159

CHAPTER IX.
AD HOMINEM ARGUMENT OF THE REVISIONISTS...... 174

CHAPTER X.
CHANGES PROPOSED IN THE COMMON VERSION 208

CHAPTER XI.
THE PORTION OF THE REVISION PUBLISHED........... 229

CHAPTER XII.
CONCLUSION 246

Preface by the Editor.

WE deeply regret the necessity which exists for the publication of such a work as the present volume. The exposure of Jesuitism, whether popish or Protestant, is a task so irksome that we instinctively shrink from its performance; but when it is needful to be done, he who performs it in a candid, charitable spirit, deserves the gratitude of all concerned. We think the author of the following pages has tempered unavoidable severity with the meekness of wisdom; and that no one can justly complain of a want of fairness and courtesy in the matter and manner, tone and temper, of his production.

The "tactics" of the immersionist translators ought to be exposed, though the exposure is humiliating to every lover of the Bible. The rampant sectarianism which is at the head and front of the movement is too palpable, and, as Mr. Lee shows, has been too often admitted, to be denied with any credit. We see, indeed, while these sheets are passing through the press, that some of the leaders in this schismatical movement are beginning to hesitate as they approach the brink of the precipice: they are afraid to take the leap, and well they might be! What if the masses for whose benefit "immersion" is to be "printed in the Bible," should learn to attach the idea of sprinkling to that term, rather than that of dipping to the mode of baptism! It is shrewdly suggested that such a thing as this would not be without precedent. And truly no one need marvel at this, for it would not be a tithe as absurd to make immersion mean affusion as to make baptism in the New Testament mean immersion.

As to the other changes proposed in the New Version, all we have to say on this subject is, that if they are amendments we do not want them in our standard Bible, unless put there by competent authority: of course, we do not want them if they are not amendments, but mere alterations, frequently for the worse—as are many of the changes that have come under our notice.

We care not how many versions and commentaries are made by learned men, provided they do not usurp the place of our old English Bible. We can tolerate an occasional correction of the authorized text in the course of a sermon, though we think this should be very seldom attempted. We sometimes hear such pulpit criticisms of the version of the forty-seven translators of our English Vulgate as remind us of the anecdote told by old Isaac Walton, in his Life of Bishop Sanderson. When Mr. Sanderson was at Lincoln College, Oxford, under the care of the learned Dr. Kilbie, one of "King James's translators," he and the learned Hebrician made a tour into Derbyshire, and being at church on a Sunday, heard a young preacher declaim against the then late translation, somewhat, it would seem, in the spirit of the immersionist revisionists. He showed, says Walton, "three reasons why a particular word should have been otherwise translated. When evening prayer was ended, the preacher was invited to the doctor's friend's house, where, after some conference, the doctor told him he might have preached more useful doctrine, and not have filled his auditors' ears with needless exceptions against the late translation; and for that word for which he offered to that poor congregation three reasons why it ought to have been translated as he said, he and others had considered all three, and found thirteen more considerable reasons why it was translated as now printed; and told him, if his friend, then attending him, should prove guilty of such indiscretion, he should forfeit his favor, — to which Mr. Sanderson said, he hoped he should not; and the preacher was so ingenuous as to say, he would not justify himself."

We are not sanguine enough to expect such ingenuousness on the part of those who are engaged in the present movement, as a blind sectarianism is the motive by which they are influenced. Nevertheless, a fair exposure of their movements and methods may keep the unsuspecting from an entangling alliance with them, if it should not be otherwise serviceable to the interests of truth and righteousness. With this view the present little book was written by the author: that its circulation will be productive of good is the belief of those who have examined it, including

The Editor

NASHVILLE, TENN., March 8, 1856.

Immersionists against the Bible.

CHAPTER I.

INTRODUCTION.

THE manner in which the New Version movement has been advocated, has had, as I conceive, a tendency to lessen the confidence of the public mind in the Divine origin and the uncorrupted preservation of the Sacred Scriptures. And, indeed, this is the necessary tendency of the movement itself. It should therefore be exposed and resisted by every lover of Divine truth. An eminent British statesman has said, that public confidence may be far more easily destroyed than restored, when once affected. A brainless fanatic may destroy in an hour a temple which required ages, and incalculable treasure, with the direction of the highest order of genius, to complete. Let the confidence of the masses of the people in the truth of the Bible be once destroyed, and what may we not expect? The scenes enacted in France, in the latter part of the last century and the beginning of the present, may be reënacted; or the state of things which has existed in the greater part of Europe, and especially in Germany, may prevail throughout Christendom,—in which, while the Bible is avowedly received as the text-book of religion, it is made to bow down in subordination to human reason. If, as the advocates of this movement contend, the version in common use is sectarian, and not to be trusted as a guide to truth and duty, in a great many cardinal respects, how much more confidence can they expect to be placed in their proposed version? And, should they succeed in destroying confidence in King James's version, how will they manage to secure confidence in their own? They will not be able to do so, unless they *can demonstrate* that they are free from *sectarian bias;* and in order to do this, they must demonstrate that they are *infallible:* that is, under the influence of *Divine inspiration.* Should they not be able to do this, and the contingency referred to should occur, what foundation will the Church have for her faith? "If the foundations be destroyed, what can the righteous do?"

Paine and Voltaire have scarcely employed more profanity in their attacks upon the sacred writings, than the most prominent advocates of this scheme have used in reference to the version in common use. They have indulged in low, vulgar abuse, which would far better become *the very lowest infidel club* than an assembly of those *calling themselves Christians.*

Indeed, they have made some of the very same objections to our translation which Paine and others of the lower class of infidels have made; and one avowed object of the movement is to endeavor to remove all ground of objection to the Holy Scriptures upon the part of infidels.

And, though these "*nibbling critics*" have generally little talent, and less learning, yet they have misled many of the unwary, and will, if not checked, do much harm to the cause of truth. It is our design, in these pages, to stop the mouths of these gainsayers.

One thing which distinguishes the advocates of the New Version movement is, their habitual (though we hope unintentional) suppression and misrepresentation of facts. They are endeavoring to make false impressions in regard to the origin of the movement, and in regard to the main object had in view. My main object in the following pages will be to present the movement in its true light, by presenting the facts in connection with its origin and history. And, in doing this, I shall not depend upon *rumor*, but I shall present extracts from authentic and reliable documents—principally those published by the American and Foreign Bible Society, the American Bible Union, and societies coördinate and subordinate to those.

I will get my authority mainly from the men who led the way in getting up the movement, and who have been mainly concerned in the prosecution of it from the beginning.

CHAPTER II.

THE ORIGIN OF THE MOVEMENT.

A GREAT outcry has been made against the American Bible Society by the advocates of the New Version movement. It is charged that the Society has treated immersionists with great injustice, in their refusal to patronize versions of the Holy Scriptures made by them, while, at the same time, they have liberally sustained, by their influence and appropriations in money, versions made by other denominations. They complain especially of the action of the Society in reference to the version in the Burmese language, made by Dr. Judson, which was the immediate occasion of their secession from the Society, and the formation of the American and Foreign Bible Society.

That the reader may see whether there be any valid ground of complaint or not, I make the following extract from the account given of this matter by the American Bible Society. (Bible Translations, pp. 4, 5, 6.)

"In July, 1835, a letter was received through a friend in Philadelphia, from the Rev. Wm. H. Pearce, an English Baptist missionary at Bengal, in India. In this letter information was given that the writer, together with the Rev. Mr. Yates, a brother missionary, had prepared a new version of the Bengalee Scriptures, which they were desirous of having published. With Christian frankness it was stated, that in this version they had translated the Greek terms *baptizo* and *baptisma* by words which signify *immerse* and *immersion*, and that the Bible Society at Calcutta had, on this account, refused to patronize it. Had this letter contained nothing further, the Board could easily have dismissed the whole matter, as they had no responsibilities connected with that version. But it was further stated that this new Bengalee translation was made on the same principles as those which obtained in the Burmese translation, which it was understood the American Bible Society patronized. Here was a new and startling announcement. The Board had indeed granted, at different times, many thousand dollars towards the publication of this Burmese version, but without information from any quarter, or the least suspicion that it was of the character described by Mr. Pearce. They knew the Rev. Dr. Judson, the translator, to be a learned and pious man, and therefore felt a confidence that he had made what they considered a *faithful* version; i. e., one which conveyed the inspired meaning—the only point to which they had thought of directing attention—presuming every friend of the Bible Society to be aware that its Board could not appropriate moneys for any new version of a marked denominational character.

"On inquiring of the Rev. S. H. Cone, (one of the Standing Committee on Distribution,) who had repeatedly solicited funds for the Burmese version, whether that version was prepared as described by Mr. Pearce, he, for the first time, informed them that such was the fact. Although this letter had been once before the Committee on Distribution, the Board, at its meeting in

August, referred it to the same committee again for further consideration. The committee, after frequent meetings, were unable to recommend any course which would satisfy all concerned. In order to give this subject the most full and impartial investigation, the Board now appointed a special committee of seven, namely : a Presbyterian, an Episcopalian, a Baptist, a Methodist, a Moravian, one of the Reformed Dutch Church, and one from the Society of Friends. After repeated meetings of this select committee, and much inquiry, they brought in a report with sundry resolutions. The Rev. S. H. Cone, one of the number, also presented a minority report. The whole subject was now postponed for a further and careful consideration. The managers were not yet disposed to adopt the resolutions submitted, as they hoped, by a prudent delay, for the adjustment of the difficulty which had arisen, in a way satisfactory to all who were interested.

"Before the next meeting of the Board, in September, several letters were received from Baptist clergymen, in whose judgment they had great regard, expressing the hope that no hasty measures would be adopted, and suggesting some changes and additions in relation to the pending resolutions, which they had seen in a Baptist paper.

"These letters were laid before the Board, and the proposed changes were made. After frequent postponements and much deliberation, (more, probably, than they ever before bestowed on any one topic,) at a special meeting in February, 1836, they adopted the following preamble and resolutions—resolutions which had been prepared, or modified, and approved of by some of the most intelligent and worthy Baptist clergymen in America:

"By the Constitution of the American Bible Society, its managers are, in the circulating of the Holy Scriptures, restricted to such copies as are 'without note or comment,' and, in the English language, to 'the version in common use.' The design of these restrictions clearly seems to have been to simplify and mark out the duties of the Society, so that all religious denominations of which it is composed might harmoniously unite in performing these duties.

"As the managers are now called to aid extensively in circulating the Sacred Scriptures in all languages other than the English, they deem it their duty, in conformity with the obvious spirit of their compact, to adopt the following resolutions as the rule of their conduct in making appropriations for the circulation of the Scriptures in all *foreign tongues.*

"*Resolved,* That in appropriating money for the translating, printing, or distributing of the Sacred Scriptures in foreign languages, the managers feel at liberty to encourage only such versions as conform in the principles of their translation to the common English version, at least so far as that all the religious denominations represented in this Society can consistently use and circulate said versions in their several schools and communities.

"*Resolved,* That a copy of the above preamble and resolutions be sent to each of the Missionary Boards accustomed to receive pecuniary aid from this Society, with a request that the same may be transmitted to their respective mission stations where the Scriptures are in process of translation; and also, that the said several Missionary Boards be informed that their applications for aid be accompanied with a declaration that the versions which they propose to circulate are executed in accordance with the above resolutions."

Now, what ground is there for the complaint of injustice, if the above be a true account? And no one has dared to say, as far as I know, that it is not a correct account.

In what light does Dr. Cone, who had repeatedly solicited funds for the Burmese version, and others connected with that enterprise, appear? Did they not know that it was being made on immersionist principles? And were they not aware that the grant of pecuniary aid was in contravention of the condition upon which the Society was originally organized; as also of the spirit of the constitution of the Society? Yet the matter was kept a profound secret. The managers say that they had been "without any information from any quarter, or the least suspicion that it was of the character described by Mr. Pearce," till they were informed by that gentleman in July, 1835. And it seems that Mr. Pearce made this disclosure incidentally. The Calcutta Bible Society having refused to patronize the translation made by himself and Mr. Yates into the Bengalee language, he was seeking aid from the American Bible Society, and, in order to succeed in his suit, he adduced the fact that they were already patronizing the Burmese version, which was made upon strictly immersionist principles. Thus, incidentally, was "the cat let out of the wallet." And what ground for the loud complaint of injustice in the final action of the Society in this case? The Society had ample ground of complaint against Dr. Cone and others, who were in the secret in regard to the character of the Burmese version, and who successfully solicited funds in aid of it, to the amount of "many thousand dollars." The Society might in justice, in conformity with the spirit and letter of the constitution, have demanded the refunding of these "many thousand dollars."

The adoption of some version which could be conscientiously used by all the denominations composing the Society, was a condition indispensable to its original organization. And, had the Board of Managers continued to patronize a version known to be strictly denominational in its character, the Society would have been annihilated in a very short time.

Although it could be proved that the Society erred in selecting the version in common use as their standard, (and this we think cannot be done,) yet there is no ground to complain of the course they pursued in this case. And yet, strange to say, they complain, and make very serious charges against the Society, which it may be proper to notice briefly.

It is objected that the Society have changed their policy—objecting to and withholding their aid from versions of such a character as they once patronized without hesitation. The reply of the Board of Managers to this is as follows: "That they never, in a single case, granted aid to a version which they knew at the time to be of such a character that only a part of their associates could consistently use it. Taking it for granted that none would ask them to aid denominational versions, they now find that in two instances they have aided such, though in honest ignorance. It appears that a small edition of an Indian Gospel was once printed by them, where *baptizo* was translated by a word which signifies to *sprinkle* or *pour;* and that one version in India has been aided where the same Greek word has been translated by a term signifying *immerse*. Had the peculiarity of these translations been known at the time, they would by no means have been encouraged."

It is charged again that the Society has acted with partiality, by allowing other denominations to make such foreign versions as they choose, while Baptists have not this privilege. The Board of Managers reply: "This charge can have no foundation, unless other denominations choose to make versions of such a character that all the members of the Bible Society can use them, while those who complain make such versions as their denomination alone can consistently use."

It is alleged again, that the managers have laid down such rules in regard to versions, as Baptist translators cannot conscientiously follow.

They reply, "That they lay down no rules which they do not consider as enjoined on them by the conditions of their union, by the framers of the Society. If these rules bear with undue pressure on any portion of the compact, it is for those who appoint the Board, and who have control of the constitution, to alter that instrument so that *men of every creed and sentiment may prepare such foreign versions as they please, with the expectation they will be published out of the common Bible fund!* At present such license would be deemed a violation of what the constitution requires."

The managers are charged with the inconsistency of patronizing German and Dutch Bibles, where *baptizo* is translated by words which signify *immerse*, and yet withholding aid from the Bengalee and Burmese Bibles translated in the same way.

The reply is, "That the German and Dutch are *ancient* 'received versions,' such as the founders of the Society promised to patronize. In the next place, the translated words alluded to, though they once signified *immerse*, have (like many words in the English Bible) lost their first meaning, and are now of as general import as the English word *baptize*. They are versions which both Baptists and Pedobaptists can and do use continually without objection. Should the versions referred to in India, as they are in the main good, undergo a similar change as to the import of a few words, so that different denominations can use them, the managers will feel no scruple in granting them patronage."

Another grave charge made against the Society is, that it has received a large amount of money from Baptists, particularly that it has received forty or fifty thousand dollars in the way of legacies, while it has made to the denomination, as such, but very partial appropriations, and now refuses to refund what is still due.

The reply of the managers to this is, "That while a part, perhaps a large part of the denomination who aid the Bible cause in any form have seceded from the American Bible Society, and formed one exclusively under denominational control, (its managers being necessarily Baptists,) yet a highly respected and valuable portion are still coadjutors with the national institution." "It would be improper, then, by returning Baptist funds, even if the alleged amount were correct, to treat the denomination as if it were no longer a part of the Bible compact.

"But the charge as to the amount is not correct. The aggregate of legacies received from Baptists, so far as known to the Board, is no more than $18,000.

"And how was this amount expended? In preparing and circulating English, German, and French Bibles for the good of our own common country; and a large debt remained after it was expended. No portion went to aid the missions of other denominations in preparing the Scriptures in any form. It cannot be asked, then, that these funds should be paid back to the complainants.

"It appears, on examining the Society's books, that while no more than $18,000 has been received from Baptist legacies, and that this was all expended at home for a common object, the Baptist Foreign Mission Society was furnished, between the years 1831 and 1838, with no less than $27,000 for the exclusive use of that denomination in preparing and circulating the Scriptures in France, Germany, Bengal, and Burmah. In addition to these grants of money, the managers made numerous donations of English and other Scriptures, for the exclusive use of Baptist missions. During the years 1838 and 1839, Messrs. Pasto and Love, Baptist missionaries in Greece, were furnished by the Society's agent in the Levant (and with great pleasure) with no less than 12,933 portions of Scripture, amounting in value to some $5000. It appears, then, that no less than $30,000 in money and books have been furnished by the Board to aid Baptist missionaries in circulating the Scriptures, while little more than half of that sum has been received from Baptist legacies; and this was received under such circumstances as to pay no part of those large grants.

"But it is said that although the $40,000 or $50,000 of legacies spoken of as *furnished* to the Society may not as yet be actually paid over, still that sum will be paid from the residuum of the estate of Mr. Marsh, according to the provisions of his will. The American Bible Society, it is true, is one of the residuary legatees of said estate. How far there is a prospect of any speedy avails from this quarter will be seen after reading the following letter from the executor:

"'Hackensack, Jan. 18th, 1840.

"'Dear Sir:—In reply to your letter of the 15th inst., respecting information of the present condition of the legacy left by the late Mr. Marsh to the American Bible Society, I have to state, that by the will of Mr. Marsh the Society, in addition to the legacy of $10,000 which has been paid, are residuary legatees in common with the grandchildren, and their children, of the eight uncles of the testator,—the Society to receive one-third, the aforesaid children the other two-thirds. These residuary legatees are very numerous, and scattered throughout England. We have ascertained about one hundred; and from information received, there are, at least, as many more, whose names we have not been able to ascertain. Proceedings have been instituted in the Court of Chancery to have the estate settled, but from various causes it has not been brought to a close; and when it will be it is impossible for me to say. I am advised that I cannot safely pay any of the residuary legatees without having them all brought in some way into court, so as to be bound by a decree, in order to a final settlement of the estate.

"'Very respectfully yours,

"'James Hague.'

"It is obvious that a long period must intervene

before this residuum (if it *ever* come) will reach the treasury. Should it ere long be received, it can with every propriety be employed, as was the $10,000 already realized from the same estate, in furnishing English, French, and German Bibles to the mixed population of our own country.

"But it is contended that in addition to the legacies in question, a large amount has been furnished by Baptists in the way of life-directorships, life-memberships, etc. Some have placed the amount of payments of this kind at $40,000 or $50,000, equal to that of the legacies received and prospective.

"Now, while the managers are greatly averse to comparisons as to contributions of different denominations, they have been led, by the repeated *charges* referred to, to examine with some care as to their accuracy. They find, in the first place, in relation to life-directors, that out of a list of more than four hundred belonging to the Society, only thirteen are of the Baptist denomination. Of these thirteen, two were constituted directors on account of having been members of the Convention which formed the Society. Four others were made directors in consequence of having been executors where legacies were left it. Two others were made directors by contributions furnished by men of other denominations; and one of the remainder is still a friend of the American Bible Society. It does not appear, then, that there are, in any view of the matter, more than the value of four directorships to be returned.

"In relation to life-members, it is not easy to determine the precise number belonging to the Baptist persuasion. In looking over a list of more than four thousand names, not more than about one hundred can be thus identified; while several of these were constituted members by those of other creeds, and several more are still friendly to the Society. But, allowing there were one hundred and fifty life-members, each of whom has contributed thirty dollars, the total would amount to no more than $4,500, to be added to the $600 for life-directorships.

"The Board have next looked over the names of the one hundred and twenty citizens in New York who aided in the erection of the Society's house, at an expense of $22,000. While they find subscriptions from almost every other denomination, they find but one (Dr. Luke Barker's) belonging to that from which these charges now come. This contribution was thirty dollars, to be added to the $5,100 above named. They look, then, at donations made specifically to aid distributions in Burmah. Presuming these to have been made by Baptists, they find them to amount in all to less than $1000. As to contributions made through auxiliaries, there are no means for determining definitely what amount has been thus received. From the large auxiliaries in New England, New York, and a few at the South, whence most of the free donations come, it is clear to the Board, from inquiry and statements of agents, that a small amount, *comparatively*, (as in the case of life-directorships, life-memberships, and the building-fund,) has ever been furnished by Baptists, particularly by those who have seceded.

"In the newly-settled States, those of that denomination have united with others in procuring and distributing Bibles in their respective counties. But here the value was returned in books, and, in many instances, large gratuitous supplies in addition. Not a few of their number continue still to aid in these domestic distributions, both to the gratification of the auxiliaries and the parent Society. Funds thus paid in for books add nothing to the capital of the institution, and can furnish no claim for a demand on those which come as free donations. While, then, it cannot be determined with minute accuracy what amount of money has been furnished by Baptists, gratuitously, or so that it can be used by other denominations, the Board have no belief that it can surpass or equal the more than $30,000 which they as a sect have received from the institution. Aside from the $18,000 of legacies, (used at home, and not to be counted,) there is no evidence of their having contributed to the treasury *one half* the amount which they have received from it. Under such circumstances, the managers cannot, of course, feel the obligation of making *further returns* to those who have chosen to leave the Society, and to assert in so many ways its wrong-doing."—*Bible Translations,* pp. 7–14.

From the foregoing exhibition of facts, it would seem strange indeed that the immersionists should complain of the injustice with which they have been treated by the American Bible Society. With what face can they complain that they were not permitted to draw from the fund contributed mainly by Pedobaptist denominations, to publish versions of the Sacred Scriptures which were made so as to express their peculiar, strange, and false views of baptism?—that the American Bible Society were unwilling to take the money contributed to publish and circulate such versions of the Holy Scriptures as they could all conscientiously use, to publish and circulate their peculiar *dogma* of "*dip, and nothing but dip?*"

They take it exceedingly hard, indeed, that they have to print at their own expense versions intended specially to sustain their peculiar notion about baptism. It would seem but reasonable that, if they are determined to take the responsibility of altering the word of God for their own accommodation, they should be willing to bear the expenses themselves, and not wish to involve others in the consequences of their temerity.

CHAPTER III.

THE MAIN DESIGN OF THE MOVEMENT.

THIS, we will prove, is the substitution of *immerse* and its cognates for *baptize* and its cognates—at least, so far as the word relates to the ordinance of baptism. It may be proper, however, before we proceed to the proofs, to place the issue involved distinctly and clearly before the mind of the reader, that he may be the better prepared to appreciate the argument.

The question to be settled is not whether there are errors in the commonly received version of the Bible. We admit this; yet we deny that they involve any doctrine or precept of Christianity. Neither is it the question, whether there ought to be a new version of the Holy Scriptures. And yet we are prepared to show, from the best authority, that there is no necessity for it.

The real question is this: *Ought there to be such a version of the Holy Scriptures as the advocates of this movement contemplate, i. e., a strictly sectarian one—one in which immerse and its cognates shall be substituted for baptize and its cognates?* THIS IS THE QUESTION. *Here is the real issue.* It is important that the reader should keep his mind steadily fixed on this point. The New Version advocates have endeavored, and are endeavoring, both in public addresses before the people, and in their publications, to mislead other denominations, and the public as well as their own people, in regard to the *main design* of the movement. They are afraid to risk it on its own merits. And the policy is to avoid public odium as far as possible, in order that they may the more certainly secure the means of prosecuting the enterprise; for it is an expensive business. And no doubt they design also to keep the real character of the movement out of view as long as possible, that they may have time to drill their own people into an acceptance of the denominational version, when it appears. They dwell largely upon the thousands of errors which they say are in King James's translation—the removal of which they urge is the object of the movement. They disclaim the sectarian character of the movement in these *"Buncombe"* productions, and assert that nearly all the Protestant denominations are united in it—that a large proportion of the translators are Pedobaptists, etc. Notwithstanding all this manœuvering, I will show that the movement, from its incipiency, has been strictly sectarian—that it was begun, and has been and is still prosecuted, for the purpose, *mainly*, of subserving sectarian views and interests—that it is designed to produce a strictly *immersionist* version—*baptize* and its cognates being rejected, and *immerse* and its cognates being substituted. And I will make this showing not from *rumor*, but mainly from official documents of the associations concerned in the movement.

The history of the movement shows this to have been the predominant idea.

In the preface to Professor Stuart's work on

Baptism, we learn that five Baptist missionaries, viz., Bennett, Jones, Judson, Kincaid, and Wade, in a letter, dated Maulmain and Rangoon, May, 1832, inquired of Professor Stuart: "Shall we transfer the Greek word βαπτίζω into the Burmese language, when it relates to the ordinance of baptism, or translate it by a word significant of *immersion*, or by a word of the same import?" He answered this inquiry, and advised them not to translate *baptizo* by *immerse*, or any other mere modal term; but to transfer it into the heathen tongues as it had been done into the Latin, French, English, etc.; and his book on Baptism was written to sustain the correctness of this advice. These missionaries, however, refused to follow this advice; and Dr. Judson, as we have already seen, proceeded to use a term in the Burmese version which signifies exclusively *to immerse*. We see, then, that the manner in which βαπτίζω should be translated was a subject of chief interest before the enterprise was entered upon. The determination to translate it by a word signifying *immerse* was no doubt formed before they consulted Professor Stuart. Nothing he could have said would in the least have changed their purpose. They were not, indeed, asking for light; but they hoped to secure the influence of Professor S., preëminently distinguished for his classical and biblical learning, in favor of the enterprise. They remind me of the case of a preacher, who, in a very serious tone, consulted a clerical brother in regard to his marriage with a certain lady. The brother consulted wished to know how far the case had progressed. "O," said he, "we are engaged." "Well," said the other, "it is too late to consult me now: why did you not consult me sooner?" "O," said the inquirer, "I was afraid some one else would get her."

The desire to get *immerse* in the place of *baptize* is clearly seen from this incident to have been at the very bottom of the whole movement. This desire has led the way in every step that has been taken from the beginning. *Immerse* is the "*head and front*" of the whole movement. It is the central idea round which every thing else revolves, and to which every thing else is subordinate. This clearly appears in the further history of the movement.

Why did the Calcutta Bible Society refuse to patronize the version in the Bengalee language made by the Rev. Messrs. Pearce and Yates? Why, exclusively on the ground that it was an *immersionist version*. Why did the American Bible Society refuse to patronize this version? and why did they resolve to cease patronizing the Burmese version made by Dr. Judson, when they learned, through the Rev. Mr. Pearce, the true character of it? Why, simply because it was a sectarian version, and they could not patronize it in accordance with the constitution. Why did the Baptists take exception to the action of the Board of Managers, and, with Dr. Cone at their head, secede from the Society, and form one of their own? It was on account of their devotion to the principle of substituting *immerse* for *baptize*. Let the Board of Managers of their own Society tell us: "Since the die is cast, and the Bible societies of Asia, Europe, and America have united in the determination neither to sanction nor patronize any version in which *baptizo* is made to signify *immerse*, what have the Baptists to do but to come up to the help of the Lord, even to the help of the Lord against the mighty?"—Quar. Pap., p. 4.

Let Dr. Cone say why the Baptists seceded from the American Bible Society, and why they organized the American and Foreign Bible Society, in his speech at the first anniversary of the American Bible Union, at New York, October 3d, 1850: "The American and Foreign Bible Society was organized to VINDICATE A PRINCIPLE; and, in accordance with this principle, *baptizo* and its cognates should be rendered by words signifying *immerse, immersion,*" etc. Did the managers know the principle upon which the secession took place? Did Dr. Cone know? Is it likely that the managers and Dr. Cone, the president of the A. and F. Bible Society for many years, were ignorant of the principle upon which the Society was organized? It is true that the A. and F. Bible Society resolved to use the commonly received version till otherwise ordered by the Society; but, at the same time, they meditated a new English version, "in which (to use their own language) the word βαπτίζω shall be *faithfully* translated *to immerse.*"

The final consideration of this project was deferred till 1850, when (the matter being before the managers) "they shrank from the responsibility of their original purpose," and decided to be content with the commonly received version of the English Scriptures. And, at the anniversary of the Society in the same year, this decision was approved and adopted by a large majority. Upon this decision, the minority, with Dr. Cone at their head again, "seceded from the secession," and formed what is styled the American Bible Union. Why were they induced to take this step? Hear Dr. Cone again upon this point, in the speech from which we quoted above. Having said, as we have quoted, "that the A. and F. Bible Society was organized to vindicate *a principle,*" and "that, in accordance with this principle, *baptizo* and its cognates should be rendered by words signifying *immerse, immersion,*" etc., he proceeds to indicate the principle which was to govern the American Bible Union: "And here (i. e., whether *baptizo* should be rendered *immerse*) we fought the battle with the Pedobaptists, and here we have to fight the battle over again with the Baptists, who will not allow *immerse, immersion,* etc., to have a place in the New Testament.

'When Greek meets Greek,
Then comes the tug of war.'

Either fear 'that the Pedobaptists will come down upon us with tremendous power,' as a distinguished brother said, or *shame,* or some other motive of which I know nothing, deters many from bearing *in English* the same testimony for Christ's despised ordinance of *immersion,* which they have made it the imperative duty of their missionaries to bear in all the languages of the heathen."

Does not the above quotation most conclusively show that the reason of Dr. Cone and his brethren's seceding from the American and Foreign Bible Society was simply that they (the Society) would not agree to have an immersionist version of the English Scriptures? Would they have been satisfied with any version which should not have conformed to this principle? It was not merely a *new version* which they wanted, that should contain a correction of errors in general, but it was a new version which should have *immerse* instead of *baptize*, in accordance with the principle announced by Dr. Cone. This was a *sine quâ non* with them. This, then, is the "*principle*," for the sake of which they separated from the A. and F. Bible Society, and upon which they organized the American Bible Union. Have they since abandoned this principle? Where is the record of it? They have never published it to the world. There is abundant proof that they intend to adhere to it with a passionate devotion. Ah! to have their favorite dogma in the New Testament! It will save them a world of trouble and vexation. It will be indeed a great acquisition. They will be

—"As rich in having such a jewel,
As twenty seas, if all their sand were pearl,
The water nectar, and the rocks pure gold."

Why did the immersionists in India and Europe secede from the Bible Society of Calcutta, and the British and Foreign Bible Society? Because these societies refused to sanction or patronize any version in which $\beta\alpha\pi\tau\iota\zeta\omega$ is made to signify *immerse*. Would they have seceded, had it not been for this? And would any thing short of a revocation of this decision have satisfied them? It would not. And this is settled beyond all controversy by the fact that they formed a society in England, subsequently to the organization of the American and Foreign Bible Society, called "The British Translation Society," one article of whose constitution reads as follows: "It shall be the object of this Society to encourage the production and circulation of complete translations of the Holy Scriptures, completely authenticated for fidelity, *it being always understood that the words relating to the ordinance of baptism shall be translated by words signifying immerse."*

This for ever settles the question as regards the main object the British Baptists have in view. Their *main* object is to put *immerse* in the place of *baptize;* and they are candid enough to avow it even in the constitution of their Society. I regret I cannot say the same of the immersionists in this country. But it may be said that the advocates of revision in this country have nothing to do with the movement in Great Britain, and are not responsible for any position they may have assumed.

But it is a fact, that the Translation Society of Great Britain was organized under the auspices of the American and Foreign Bible Society, the managers of which appointed Dr. McClay, in September, 1839, to visit the Baptists of England. And, in a letter addressed to them, they give their reasons for sending their agent.

I make the following extracts : "While it is our sincere prayer that the appointment of brother McClay may promote a more intimate fraternal union between British and American Baptists in every thing that relates to the prosperity of the Redeemer's kingdom, we particularly hope that in the publication of *faithful* versions of the Bible in all lands, we may ere long obtain the active coöperation of every Baptist in Great Britain. Why should they not thus unite, when it is known that the British and Foreign Bible Society and the American Bible Society have virtually combined to obscure at least a part of Divine revelation? To the friends of truth it cannot be otherwise than a subject of deep lamentation that these societies, which, of all others, ought to be anti-sectarian, continue to circulate versions of the Bible *unfaithful,* at least so far as the subject of *Baptism* is concerned."—Third Annual Report, pp. 45, 46.

In these extracts, Dr. McClay is recognized as the agent of the Society; and the managers express the hope that he may influence them (the English Baptists) to coöperate "in the publication of *faithful versions* of the Bible." And we learn what they mean by "faithful versions" in their lamentation about the course pursued by the B. and F. B. Society and the A. B. Society in circulating "versions of the Bible *unfaithful, at least so far as the subject of baptism is concerned.*" Here is more than a hint as regards the principle upon which they expected the English Baptists to coöperate with them. They were expected to recognize *immersion* as a *sine quâ non* in versions of the Bible.

Dr. McClay, after visiting the Baptist churches generally, writes to the American and Foreign Bible Society from London, as follows: "It is proposed to organize a Translation Society," etc. (Quar. Pap., p. 122.) In the next letter he writes as follows: "My mission to Great Britain, by the Divine blessing, has been crowned with success. It has aided in the formation of the Bible Translation Society, whose object is to promote the circulation of *faithful versions* of the Sacred Scriptures in all languages." And what he means by such "versions," we learn from what he says of the British and Foreign Bible Society: "A society that has treated us with injustice and contempt, and by their actions say that they would rather see the heathen perish in their idolatry, ignorance, and unbelief, than give them a Bible that shall inform them of the exact mind of the Holy Spirit on the subject of *baptism.*" And this Society (the British Translation Society) was formed to promote this end—i. e., to do what the B. and F. Bible Society had failed to do, and were unwilling to do—inform the heathen of "the exact mind of the Holy Spirit on the subject of *baptism.*"

To show more fully that the societies in England and America are *one* in their position on the subject of a new version, the managers of the American and Foreign Bible Society, speaking of the success of their agent in the formation of the Translation Society, use the following language:

"Your Board consider as auspicious in the history of our denomination the union of American and British Baptists in one common effort to give to the remotest nations the revelations of Infinite Wisdom, unadulterated by any admixture of human superstition." (Third Annual Report, pp. 11, 39, 41.)

Here is a hearty and unqualified approval of the Bible Translation Society of Great Britain. They speak of the "union of British and American Baptists" in the translation movement. But how could this be if they did not agree in the great cardinal principle? In the appendix to the Third Annual Report, p. 65, the managers publish the entire constitution of the Translation Society, embracing the second article which we have quoted above. In their Fourth Report, p. 65, they welcome the institution in the following terms:

"The formation of this Society on the 24th of March, 1840, has imparted joy to our hearts, and vigor to our hopes concerning the speedy accomplishment of that great object for which the American and Foreign Bible Society was constituted."

The American and Foreign Bible Society fully approved of the action of the Board in every step they took in reference to this Society. At their anniversary, April 29th, 1841, the following resolution was unanimously passed:

"*Resolved*, That we rejoice in the recent formation of the Bible Translation Society in Great Britain, and hail it as an institution kindred to the American and Foreign Bible Society, and a valuable coadjutor in the Bible translation." (Fourth Annual Report, p. 60.)

How could this Society be "kindred" to the American and Foreign Bible Society, "and a valuable coadjutor in the work of Bible translation," if they did not agree in their position in regard to the translation of *baptizo?*

In the Fifth Annual Report, p. 8, Dr. Cone, adopting the language of the secretary of the British Translation Society, says: "Our only business is to uphold *immersionist* versions, and give them as large a circulation as we can; and this becomes our business, because all the rest of the Christian world have thrown them away. This single object is our rallying-point. In these sentiments," says Dr. Cone, "we cordially unite."

I fear I may weary the reader with the number of quotations. But there are so many "*twistings and turnings*" adopted in order to evade the true issue, and blind the public mind, that there is required "line upon line, and precept upon precept." The course adopted by the advocates of this movement reminds me of the stratagem adopted by Cacus in stealing the cattle of Hercules, and conducting them to his cave. He led them by the *tail* instead of the *horns*, so that, if pursued, the pursuer, if he followed the *track*, might be sure to go the wrong way, and arrive at the wrong place.

All the sophistry they can invent is employed to keep the public in the dark as to what they are really about; and so "they wrap it up," to use one of their own favorite quotations. But they cannot impose upon the public where the facts are known. Neither can they restrain the indignation "that will come down upon them with tremendous power" when the facts shall generally go abroad. They

> "May as well forbid the mountain pines
> To wag their high tops and make no noise
> When they are fretted with the gusts of heaven."

CHAPTER IV.

THE MAIN DESIGN, CONTINUED.

This will appear still more fully from additional quotations from the publications of the American and Foreign Bible Society, and the American Bible Union, etc. And let the reader bear in mind what we announced in a former chapter, that we shall quote from *the publications of the friends and advocates of this movement to sustain our position.* They cannot object to this testimony. It is their own.

I first make additional quotations from the documents of the American and Foreign Bible Society. Rev. E. Kincaid, missionary to China, in a letter to the Society, says: "It appears to me that the Baptists were driven out of the old societies unless they would pledge themselves to betray Christ — unless they would barter for money *the great initiatory ordinance of the gospel.* Why keep back from the nations any part of God's word? Certainly there is no more doubt about the meaning of the word βαπτίζω than there is about ἄρτος; and to leave either untranslated, would be evidence of ignorance or dishonesty." (Quar. Pap., p. 77.)

Rev. Mr. Cushman, in a speech before the Society, says: "It (the English Bible) is not sufficiently defective, except in relation to *baptism* and church order, to be distrusted as a guide to truth and duty." (Second Annual Report, Appendix, p. 50.)

Rev. Dr. Judson: "I rejoice in the formation of the Bible Translation Society of England, and in the continued prosperity of the American and Foreign Bible Society. I verily believe that it was by the special providence of God that the old Bible societies were left to take the unjustifiable course they did, in order that *the peculiar truths* which distinguish the Baptist denomination might be brought forward in a manner unprecedented, and ultimately triumph." (Fourth Annual Report, p. 67.)

The Board of Managers use the following language: "The evils which have accrued from the introduction of a single word imposed by foreign influence, and the bigotry of an earthly prince, no human mind can compute. Nearly all the European versions subsequently made have been conformed to the principles adopted by King James's translators; and thus a word has been perpetuated from generation to generation, the precise meaning of which none but the learned could with certainty ascertain. And as these versions have, in most instances, been made by Pedobaptists, the error of sprinkling has obtained the blind and almost universal suffrage of what is called the Christian world."

The managers quote with approbation the following from Dr. Judson: "Had the Greek word *baptizo*, which denotes the principal action in this ordinance, *been translated* in the English version of the New Testament, there would probably have been among English readers no dispute concerning its import. . . . But, unhappily, our translators have retained the original word, and contented themselves with merely changing its termination." (Quar. Pap., p. 5.)

The President of the Society, Dr. Cone, says, in his address to the Society in 1846: "In retaining *baptizo*, they have done more injury to the cause of God and truth than if they had retained a dozen other old ecclesiastical words."

The Board of Managers say: "It is well known that there was not one Baptist among the forty-seven translators appointed by King James, and that we have never acknowledged that their version of the Scriptures was in all respects faithful. In common with other Christians, we have been willing to receive it only because that hitherto we had supposed that the time had not come to attempt an improved and faithful version, well knowing that in such an undertaking we must stand alone, and could hope for no assistance from Pedobaptists, whose denominational existence depends upon the *non-translation* of those words in the New Testament which relate to the ordinance of baptism." (Second Annual Report, pp. 12, 13.)

Rev. Dr. Dowling, in a speech before the American and Foreign Bible Society, says: "The principle on which the American and Foreign Bible Society is based is destined ultimately to batter down the last pillar of Popery—infant sprinkling. Protestantism says: Tell the people what God says: translate his book, that the people may know what he says: translate the whole of it, and translate it faithfully. Time will show how long the substitution of sprinkling for believers' baptism will stand before the burning torch of truth and the light of God's word, when fully and faithfully translated." (Ibid, pp. 55, 56.)

Dr. McClay, in his Saratoga address, says: "The difficulty which separated the Baptists and Pedobaptists in the Bible cause originated in the East Indies. The Pedobaptists, who came into the field long after our Baptist brethren, experienced difficulties in making converts to sprinkling, and in retaining them after they were made, in consequence of the word *baptizo* being rendered by a word signifying *immerse* in all our versions of the Scriptures."

Dr. McClay, in this same address, says: "We had no hand in making our English version. It was made for us by Episcopalians; and though we consider it in the main an excellent version, yet we believe that great injustice has been done to the truth of God by concealing the meaning of *baptism* from the unlearned, who are the mass of the community. But the day may come, and perhaps it is at no great distance, when the Baptist denomination shall deem it their duty to give a version of the Sacred Scriptures in the English language, in which the word *baptizo* shall be *faithfully* translated *to immerse,* and thus give the truth, the whole truth, and nothing but the truth in reference to this subject, that the unlearned as well as the learned may know the will of God and their duty."

Hear Dr. Cone and Mr. Wyckoff, in a tract entitled *"The Bible Translated."* "Let a

Bible Society, like the American and Foreign, dare to say that *baptizo* means *to immerse*, and stamp their conviction upon the English Testament, and a stimulus would be given to the inquiry, and a sanction to the truth, which would multiply manifold the numbers of those *immersed* into the name of the Father, and the Son, and Holy Spirit."

I might give ten times the amount of the above quotations from the publications of the American and Foreign Bible Society; but these must suffice in this place. And what do they most satisfactorily establish? Do they not show that, from the beginning, there has been but one *main idea*, and THAT *the substitution of immerse* for baptize? What is the grand objection urged against our translation? It is not objected to so much for errors in general. The capital objection is, that βαπτίζω was not translated *immerse*. Thus Dr. McClay: "Though we consider it in the main *an excellent version*, yet we believe that great injustice has been done to the truth of God by concealing *the true meaning of baptism* from the unlearned." That is, the commonly received version would do very well if it were only right on the subject of *baptism*. Their hope of the destruction of the errors of sprinkling and infant baptism, and all the corruptions existing in Pedobaptist Churches, (and these are many, according to their notion,) and the conversion of the world in the triumph of immersionist principles, is suspended upon putting *immerse* in the New Testament in the place of *baptize*.

I will now call the attention of the reader to a few additional quotations from the publications of the American Bible Union. This Society, the reader will bear in mind, is a *secession* from the American and Foreign Bible Society, (Baptist,) as *that* is a secession from the American Bible Society. And that while, in common with the American and Foreign Bible Society, it seeks to secure only *immersionist versions* of the Scriptures in foreign languages, it at the same time aims to secure a version upon this principle in

English. The friends of this Society, however, deny that such is its object, or, at least, that this is its *main design.* If, however, Dr. Cone knew any thing of the main object of the movement, such is the character of the version they seek. Dr. Cone headed the secession from the American Bible Society, and was, till the secession from the American and Foreign Bible Society, in 1850, the President of that institution; and he was the President of the American Bible Union from its organization, in 1850, till his death in 1855. No man, therefore, could enjoy better opportunity of knowing the main design of the movement than Dr. Cone did.

We have already quoted from his speech at the first anniversary of the American Bible Union, in 1850, in which he addresses his brethren as " Brethren and friends of *immersionist versions* of the Holy Scriptures in all languages, but especially *in the English.*" Now here the terms in which he addresses his brethren show the main purpose of their organization. They are addressed as "friends of *immersionist versions* of the Holy Scriptures—*especially in English.*" Did he not know whom he was addressing?

Hear Dr. Cone again, in his speech at the second anniversary of the American Bible Union, October 2d, 1851: "Brethren and friends, the American Bible Union has a mission of grave responsibility. We are called in the providence of God to employ our best efforts to *procure, print, and circulate faithful versions of the Scriptures in all lands.*"

And we learn what Dr. C. means by *faithful* versions a little further along in the same speech. Hear him: "He (Dr. C.) has dared to say from this pulpit again and again, that Christian *baptism is immersion only;* and that if right to preach it, it is right *to print* it—TO PRINT IT IN THE BIBLE; for if it is not in the Bible, we have no right *to preach* it *or print* it as a part of God's revealed will to man."

"One of the most specious arguments that has been advanced against the correction of the common version is, that thereby we must forfeit the name of *Baptists*. The words relating to the ordinance must of necessity be translated; and because the common people will learn that it is the duty of believers to be *immersed,* therefore the term *Baptist* will cease to be the appellation of those who follow their Lord. This is not a necessary consequence. . . . The great thing is to follow Christ. . . . To do this we must know what he commands. Does he command believers in Christ to be immersed in his name? Where is the difference in criminality between *printing* it and *preaching* it? If the latter be right, the former cannot be wrong." "How strange, how inexplicable, that any *who wear this name* should be afraid or ashamed *to print* what they believe and *preach!*"

"Since the English word *baptize,* according to our standard lexicographers, means to *sprinkle, pour, asperse, christen,* etc., the American Bible Union must come up to the help of the Lord against the mighty; take off the popish cover from his *pure* word; disabuse the public mind, led astray by doctors and dictionaries; and, among other revealed truths, show to all who understand our language that *baptism* is *immersion* only."

Here "the main design" is boldly avowed and defended. If they should lose their name by substituting *immerse* for *baptize*, (though not "a necessary consequence," as he thinks,) yet they must not be deterred. "The great thing is to follow Christ." "If it is right *to preach* it, (*immersion*,) it is right *to print* it." And inasmuch as it is not in the Bible, "IT IS RIGHT TO PRINT IT IN THE BIBLE:" otherwise "it is not right to *preach* it, or *print* it."

And, then, as the standard lexicographers are all wrong in the definitions they give to *baptize*, therefore "the American Bible Union must come up to the help of the Lord against the mighty," and show to those speaking our language who "are led astray by doctors and dictionaries, *that baptism is immersion only*," I would suggest that they take into consideration the propriety of attempting a new version of the "*Doctors and Dictionaries.*" If they could get them reformed to their notions, a great deal of trouble would be obviated in the prosecution of the enterprise in which they are engaged. The fact is, a new version of almost every thing will have to be secured before our immersionist friends can get along as they desire.

Listen to Dr. Cone again, in his address before the Bible Union, October 6th, 1853 : "In revising the commonly received English version, the real point of controversy between us and the anti-revisionists is the question *whether baptizo shall be translated or not.* Settle that point on the side of the truth : allow the real meaning of the word to appear in all its plainness and simplicity, and then no one but a Roman Catholic will object to the whole Bible being brought as near the original as possible."

Now, supposing Dr. Cone to have been posted in regard to the main design of the movement, this quotation settles the question.

In order that I may show that the main design on account of which the movement was begun has not been abandoned, I make a few extracts from the Bible Union Reporter for January, 1854. This is one of the organs of the Union. I quote from pages 81, 82. In a speech delivered before the American Bible Union, by the Rev. J. H. Chandler, a missionary to Siam, he gives an account of a late translation of the Scriptures into the Siamese language, by a Mr. Jones. He says that in this version, "In speaking of John the forerunner of Christ, he is called 'John the *immerser;*' and in all those passages where *baptize, baptized, baptism* occur, *immerse, immersed, immersion* are used: so that the word *Baptist* is nowhere to be found in the book: no, not even on the English title-page."

"However others may be liable to the charge of making *Baptist* Bibles and Testaments, I am sure it cannot be brought against Mr. Jones; for you will see that there is nothing about *Baptists* in any part of his translation. The converts in Siam do not, so far as I am aware, know that there is such a body as the *Baptist* denomination." ! ! !

He then gives a few extracts from the Siamese

version—Matt. iii. 1 : "In those days came John the *immerser.*" Matt. iii. 11 : "I indeed *immerse* you in water; but He will *immerse* you in the Holy Spirit and fire."

The editor of the Reporter adds: "By these extracts from our Siamese version, it will be seen that *the principles for which the Bible Union is contending, are the same* which control Baptist missionaries in Asia." The *principles* recognized by the Baptist missionary in Siam, *controlled* him to use a word for βαπτίζω which means *immerse,* and nothing else. And if this is the *same* principle for which the Bible Union is contending, then it will *control* them to put *immerse* in the place of *baptize* in their proposed new version of the English Scriptures.

I quote again from a speech delivered by the Rev. John L. Waller, LL.D., before the Revision Association, at Nashville, Tenn., April 10th, 1854, as published in the Bible Union Reporter for May, 1854, pp. 152, 153 : "The word (*baptism*) has no *modal* signification. In this respect it means any thing and every thing, and therefore *nothing.* It is a word of no mode at all. It is in vain for my Baptist brethren to tell me that *immersion* is plainly taught in the English version. I grant that it is. A child may read it there as if written in lines of light. But it is not taught by the word *baptize.* That word bears no testimony on the subject. It is as silent as an Egyptian mummy.

"It is in vain to reason with the individual who seriously insists that *baptize* means to *immerse;* or that it has any *modal* meaning whatever, since the Elizabethan age. We might as well attempt to teach logic to an orang-outang as to impart the laws of language to the man who would gravely dispute a position so self-evident. Such an individual is surely delivered over to believe a lie."

If the above be correct reasoning, what is the only alternative? Why, according to the "*principle*" which the American and Foreign Bible Society was organized "*to vindicate,*" and which the American Bible Union, as the successor of the American and Foreign Bible Society, as far as the English Scriptures are concerned, are most solemnly pledged to vindicate, they must substitute *immerse*. And is not the Revision Association, before which this address of Dr. W. was delivered, coördinate with the American Bible Union? Are not its friends coöperating with the Union in "the greatest enterprise of the age?" Have they ever disclaimed its great principle? Nay, verily; but, on the contrary, they have affirmed it in the most conclusive manner. And yet, many of the advocates of the movement positively deny that the main design is to substitute *immerse* for *baptize*. How strange, that men professing *honesty*, let alone *godliness*, should be guilty of such *shuffling!*

But listen to the following, from Tract No. 13, written by the Rev. Mr. Judd, and published by the American Bible Union: "Editors and their correspondents, and many other teachers in Israel, have taken much pains to make the people believe that the great object of the American Bible Union, and of the whole revision enterprise, is to substitute the word *immerse* for *baptize*, in our common version. . . . But the idea has no foundation in fact. It has been formed in direct opposition to the public official documents and uniform action of the Union." And then, in order to sustain this disclaimer, he gives the rules by which the translators of the new version are bound:

"1. The exact meaning of the inspired text, as that text expressed it to those who understood the original Scriptures at the time they were first written, must be translated by corresponding words and phrases, so far as they can be found in the vernacular tongue of those for whom the version is designed, with the least possible obscurity or indefiniteness.

"2. The common English version must be made the basis of revision, and all unnecessary interference with the established phraseology shall be avoided; and only such alterations shall be made as the exact meaning of the inspired text and the existing state of the language may require."

And then, after commenting on these rules, he says: "It must be seen, therefore, that the Bible

Union have never joined issue with their opponents on this point, as constituting any essential or determined part in the grand enterprise of revision."

Now, we consider the inference thus drawn from the rules as by no means legitimate; for, although they do not in so many words require the substitution of *immerse* for *baptize*, yet they do not prohibit it directly or indirectly; and the translators may therefore put *immerse* in the place of *baptize* in perfect conformity with the rules. And that this will be done is inferred from a quotation from Dr. Kendrick, in this very tract, as authority for the revision movement: "It is thought that the English Scriptures are understood on the subject of *baptism*. This is a mistake. The few who are acquainted with Baptist principles understand them; but the mass of the people do not. A translation of the word *baptizo*, and a general circulation of the Scriptures with such a translation, would do more than all other books to enlighten the masses on the subject."

How does the positive denial above quoted and this quotation, setting forth one main object of the movement, agree together? Let the candid reader determine.

Take another specimen of the game of Jesuitism they are trying to play in their effort to evade the main issue.

Dr. Williams, of New York, one of the most eminent Baptist ministers in the world, wrote, in behalf of his church, a letter to the American Bible Union, in reply to a request sent the church by the Union "for prayer and aid." The letter is published in Tract No. 10, by the Union, in connection with their reply to it through Dr. Cone and others. Here is Dr. Williams's opinion of "*the main design.*"

"The alteration most sought by some esteemed brethren among you was in the word describing the first ordinance of the Christian Church. And by laying down, as your Society is said by its friends and officers to have laid it down, that the rendering of the Greek word for *baptism* by another one is no longer held 'an open ques tion,' but that, in effect, *immerse* must take the place of *baptize*, does not your enterprise incur the very censure which your advocates cast upon King James for his instructions to translators? You limit the consciences and restrain the unfettered judgment of your revisors."

Here is the answer of the Bible Union to this, with Dr. Cone's name to it as chairman of the committee who drew it up: "To say that we limit the consciences and restrain the unfettered judgment of our revisors, . . . is to assert what you cannot prove, and to testify to what you have no reason to believe. . . . Your charge against the Bible Union on this point is as unfounded as it is unjust; and we cannot resist the conviction that the cause which arrays its ablest advocates, armed with bold assertions, against the plain documentary evidence of undeniable facts, must be at war with truth."

But, strange to say, in the same tract in which this language is used, they most clearly admit all that Dr. Williams has charged. Dr. Williams in his letter had quoted Dr. Carson against revision.

They quote from Dr. Carson, in order to show that he was in favor of it, as follows: "Luke xi. 38. He says, 'The passage there ought to have been translated—"And when the Pharisee saw it, he marvelled that he was not immersed before dinner."' Speaking of Mark vii. 4, where our version has, 'Except they *wash* they eat not,' Carson says it ought to have been translated, 'Except they *dip* themselves they eat not.' And what our version renders '*washings*,' he says ought to be translated '*immersions.*' Speaking of those who understand only the English language, he says, 'They do not understand the original, and the adoption of the words *baptize* and *baptism* can teach them nothing. Translators, by adopting the Greek word, have contrived to hide the meaning from the unlearned.'"

Here they adduce Carson as in favor of revision; but how is Carson in favor of revision, if, as they say, the putting of *immerse* in the place of *baptize* constitutes no part of the revision enterprise? for all they quote from Carson relates to that very thing. Out of their own mouths, therefore, I prove that the disclaimer above quoted is utterly false.

Again, in the same series of Tracts, No. 6, entitled, "The Bible Union's plan of Revision vindicated," by J. W. Lynd, D. D., the author shows the importance and necessity of revision by exhibiting the benefits which will flow from it. One among the number of these "*benefits*" (?) is, according to Dr. Lynd, that *immerse* will take the place of *baptize*. Hear him:

"I will give another instance in the word '*baptize.*' There can be no doubt that this word, in English religious literature, has become *generic*. It would be time lost, on this occasion, to argue this point with any one who may be bold enough to deny it. The word is currently used for sprinkling by the largest part of the Christian world. It may be said that this is a wrong use of the word; but that does not change the fact. Baptists use it to signify immersion only; but Baptists cannot change the literature of English Christendom. I ought, perhaps, to except a few, who hold that *baptizo* has no representative in the English language, and that it does not mean *to purify*, *to sprinkle*, *to pour*, or *to immerse*, but *to baptize*. With this exception, the Baptist opponents of revision, among all evangelical Christians of this country, stand alone as to the definitiveness of the English word *baptize*. All the Pedobaptists, all revisionists, regard its present use as *generic*. And yet, most strange to say, they wish to retain *baptize*, and restore its original meaning, not perceiving their own full admission that its present use is *generic*.

"If the Greek word *baptizo* mean *immerse*—if the authority of good scholarship is on this side, the English reader should have the benefit of such a rendering, and those who practice differently should have the privilege of sustaining their practice by their own opinion of the original word.

"Let such a revision, sustained by proper authority, go forth to the world, and the design of the ordinance will be more clearly seen. As that is understood, it will sweep away the error of baptizing unconscious babes. 'Buried with him by immersion into death,' will then express to the minds of men what before they could not conceive."

What does this extract show? Certainly that *baptize* is to be turned out of the New Testament, because it is *a generic* word; and *immerse* must be put in its place, because it is *specific*.

Is it likely that Dr. Lynd is ignorant of the design of the movement?

It will be satisfactory to give quotations from eminent Baptist ministers who are opposed to this movement. And it is a remarkable fact that the large majority of the most learned and gifted ministers of the Baptist Church in this country, and perhaps in Europe, are most violently opposed to this movement. This fact of itself should have great influence with Baptists as regards the merits of the movement.

In a pamphlet written by John Dowling, D.D., and entitled "*The Old-fashioned Bible*," he uses the following language: "Various other corrections of the text have been recommended in the proposed 'New Version.' Believing, however, most firmly as I do, that these suggestions have been put in only as *makeweights*, in order to aid the great object of the substitution of 'immerse' for 'baptize,' I shall not on the present occasion enter into any examination of the correctness of these criticisms."—p. 10.

"I shall now proceed, therefore, to state my reasons why we should oppose the publication, by this great denominational Society, [the American and Foreign Bible Society,] of a version of the English Scriptures, the distinguishing feature of which should be the substitution of *immerse* for *baptize* wherever it occurs in the New Testament."—p. 13.

Dr. Dowling gives as the fourth reason why he is opposed to a new version with the word *immerse* substituted for *baptize*, "Because the word *baptize is itself, to all intents and purposes, an English word.*"—p. 20.

"But turn the words *baptize*, and *baptism*, and *Baptist* out of the Bible, and what becomes of the authority for our name? We are Baptists no longer, for we repudiate the very word; nor can we with the slightest show of consistency expel the word from our Bible, and then cling to it as the name of our denomination.

"Once more, then, I repeat, if you expel this word from your Bible you must give up the name of your sect; and if you refuse to do this, other denominations will do it for you. You must call yourselves Immersers; or if that, too, is rejected because it is a transferred word, then you must call yourselves Dippers."—pp. 32, 33.

Rev. Dr. Fuller says: "The moment we resort to a new translation, we sacrifice the whole argument, and virtually say, as the book now is we cannot make out our cause: we must, therefore, follow the Campbellites, and the Socinians, and others, and make a Bible to suit ourselves."

Rev. Dr. Malcolm, as quoted by Dr. Dowling: "Were I to utter all the objections which occur to me as to the proposed 'Version,' (!) I should want a week for it. When the world is allowed to say that *we needed*, as Baptists, a New Version, to sustain ourselves, then is our right arm broken in the fight. I can add no more than to say, 1 shall spurn from me the proposed publication, and the Society which gives it birth."

Rev. Dr. Hague says: "If we should accomplish the proposed purpose, and change the word *baptize* into *immerse*, and should win the suffrages of the world, in a few years we should have to do the same thing, and make new changes."

I might add many additional quotations from the most distinguished Baptist ministers in the world, in which they express their unqualified opposition to the movement; and the prime reason of their opposition is declared to be that the design of the movement is to put *immerse* in the New Testament in the place of *baptize*, and that this is the *main* design.

The disclaimer of the main design contained in the extract we have made from Tract No. 10, containing Dr. Williams's letter against revision, and the reply of the Bible Union to that letter, was drawn up by Dr. Cone as chairman of the committee. The reader will have seen that Dr. Williams is substantially charged with falsehood in saying that the main design of the movement is to put *immerse* in the place of *baptize*. Now, in what light does this disclaimer place Dr. Cone and the Union?

This same Dr. Cone said, in 1842, "Our only business is to uphold immersionist versions. This single object is our rallying-point."

This same Doctor said, in 1849, "Let a Bible Society like the American and Foreign dare to say that *baptizo* means to *immerse*, and stamp their conviction upon the New Testament," etc.

The same gentleman, in 1850, before the American Bible Union: "Brethren and *friends of immersionist* versions of the Scriptures *in all languages, and especially in the English*, the American and Foreign Bible Society was organized to vindicate *a principle:* . . . in accordance with this *principle, baptizo* should be rendered by words signifying *immerse, immersion*," etc.

The same man, in 1851: "The American Bible Union must come up to the help of the Lord against the mighty; . . . and show to all who understand our language, that baptism is IMMERSION ONLY. . . . If it is right to preach it, it is right *to print it*—TO PRINT IT IN THE BIBLE."

The same person, in 1852: "Having directed their missionaries among the heathen to translate *baptizo* and its cognates by words signifying *immerse*, immersion, etc., they cannot be so inconsistent as to despise or reject *immersion* in their own vernacular tongue."

Hear him in 1853: "In revising the commonly received version, the real point of controversy between us and the anti-revisionists is the question whether *baptizo* shall be translated or not."

And yet, this same Dr. S. H. Cone assists in getting up a paper in reply to Dr. Williams, and puts his name to it as chairman, and sends it abroad to the world, denying most absolutely what he has so often, and in so many different forms, declared most positively and unequivocally to be true!

And Dr. Cone is not peculiar among the advocates of this, "the greatest enterprise of the age," for this "*blowing hot and cold out of the same mouth.*" It is a distinctive feature in the *tactics* of the movement. It affords a most impressive illustration of the recklessness into which even good men may be led in the advocacy of an ultra measure.

A good cause does not need such expedients. It will always be prejudiced by their adoption. The cause which demands such aid must be a bad one. Truth suffers nothing by being fully and fairly exposed. On the contrary, it will always be the gainer by such exposure. Men who are satisfied of the goodness of their cause are naturally inclined to defend it on its own merits. They will not be afraid to do so. They will prefer such a course, as a matter of policy, if for nothing else. If these sentiments be correct, we infer that the revision movement is a bad cause, and that its advocates have not full confidence in it. They do not expect to succeed by a fair and candid course. They consequently do not attempt it.

In reading their publications, it is very evident

that they were much more candid in announcing the main design in the outset of the movement than at present. Public sentiment came down upon them "with such tremendous power" that they became frightened; and they have deemed it good policy to change the mode of operation, so as to keep the main design more in the background; and the jesuitical course now adopted is the result.

"The old-fashioned Bible," as we still have it, very justly declares that "He that doeth truth cometh to the light, that his deeds may be made manifest that they are wrought in God." But "Every one that doeth evil hateth the light, neither cometh to the light, lest his deeds should be reproved."

The fact is, as is apparent to every one acquainted with the history of this movement, it is a last resort to sustain the *sinking* cause of *immersion*. The advocates of "dip and nothing but dip" have found that the commonly received version does not sustain them; and therefore they must either give up this strange dogma, and others connected with it, or they must have a new version. They must have a Bible to suit themselves, as other fanatical ultraists have. They acknowledge that the Bible, the dictionaries, the commentaries, the doctors, and a majority of the so-called Christian world, are against them; and they are constrained to do something; and the plan is to begin by reforming the Bible; and then, perhaps, they will proceed to reform every thing else that does not accord with their peculiar notion of "dip, and nothing but dip." They have truly a Herculean task before them; but then, what cannot men do with but *one single idea* to tax their powers?

CHAPTER V.

THE TACTICS OF THE MOVEMENT.

An expedient adopted by the advocates of this movement is the representation that a large number of the learned men (?) engaged in the work of revision are Pedobaptists. The design of this is to make the impression that the movement is catholic and not sectarian. And this statement is made so as to make the impression upon those not posted up in the matter, not that individuals belonging to Pedobaptist Churches, upon their own individual responsibility, are in the employ of the American Bible Union as revisors, but that they are thus engaged by the countenance and even approval of the Churches to which they belong. And these statements are made not merely by the subordinate and inferior apologists of the movement, but even by the leaders in the enterprise, and by the American Bible Union itself officially.

I quote the following from a speech of the Rev. J. S. Backus, delivered before the American Bible Union at its fifth anniversary, 1855, (Bible Union Reporter, p. 91,) and of course endorsed and published by the Union:

"I like the revision movement, because of its non-sectarian character.

"All denominations of Christians would not unite to revise the Scriptures, and no one denomination could have undertaken it alone, without exciting the jealousy of others, and having all their prejudices arrayed against the work as a sectarian thing, however faithfully done. But the Bible Union movement is not a denominational movement," etc.

Now, let the reader recur to the mass of evidence already adduced, proving most conclusively the falsity of this statement, and he will have an exhibition of a case of as unscrupulous and glaring effrontery as was ever practiced in the whole history of Jesuitism. Sometimes they strive to make the impression that all denominations of Christians are united in the movement; and then none—not even their own—is engaged in it!

Listen to the following from the Union's "Address for Prayer and Aid," signed by Dr. Cone as President, and published in the Bible Union Reporter for January, 1854: "Distinguished scholars are employed by the American Bible Union in the revision of the common version, holding their ecclesiastical connections with eight denominations: *Church of England; Old School Presbyterians; Disciples, or Reformers; Associate Reformed Presbyterians; Seventh-Day Baptists; American Protestant Episcopalians; Baptists; German Reformed Church.*

"Written contracts have been made with more than twenty scholars; and many of these, in compliance with the stipulations, have made engagements with others to work with them, so that the number of scholars actually engaged in the service of the Union does not vary far from forty.

"More than half the work already done has

been performed by scholars not connected with immersionist denominations; and we anticipate that this will hold true until the New Testament is finished.

"Seven of the revisors under written contract reside in Great Britain, and three of these are connected with the Church of England."

In the Reporter of April, 1855, I find the Methodist Church in the list of the Churches from which the translators are selected.

The design of the publication from which the above extract is taken, is to make the impression that the movement is not denominational or sectarian, but that all the evangelical denominations are engaged in it, as well as some that are not evangelical.

There is no intimation that though individuals from nine denominations are engaged as translators, yet only in the case of those from the Baptists, Disciples, and Seventh-Day Baptists, can any one of them represent the denomination to which he belongs. And the fact, therefore, that they have translators from these six Pedobaptist denominations does not affect in the slightest degree the *sectarian* IMMERSIONIST character of the movement. For who began the movement? Baptists and Campbellites. Who have been the officers of the American and Foreign Bible Society, and of the American Bible Union, up to this time? Why, none but Baptists and Campbellites. And, therefore, these Pedobaptist translators are employed by Baptists and Campbellites to do their work. They "are employed under written contract." They are getting well paid, perhaps, for the work they are doing.

But let us see what Dr. Cone thought about getting Pedobaptist aid in 1839. Listen to him: "Well knowing that in such an undertaking we must stand alone, and could hope for no assistance from Pedobaptists, whose denominational existence depends upon the *non-translation* of those words in the New Testament which relate to the ordinance of baptism."

According to the "Address for Prayer and Aid," Dr. Cone did not *know* so well as he thought he did when he uttered this language.

He thought in 1839 that the immersionists must stand alone. Now he finds men from six of the Pedobaptist denominations standing side by side with the Union; yea, are actually employed *under written contract* in doing the great work of revision! Indeed, they are destined to do the greater part of it! Well, indeed, the state of things is much better than could have been expected. But how are we to account for this wonderful result? Have these worthy Pedobaptist divines and scholars found that they can engage in this work without demolishing the denominational existence of the Churches to which they belong? Have they become convinced that they can assist in making the immersionists a Bible to suit them, and yet compromise no principle—especially as they are getting *good salaries* for their learned and pious labor? Or is it a fact, that their pecuniary necessities are so pressing that they are reconciled to dispense with *conscience* and *principle* for a season, that they may make a little to save them from want? Here is a difficulty which the ethics we have learned from "*the old-fashioned Bible"* will not enable us to solve favorably to these Pedobaptist translators, we fear, with the light we have in regard to their case.

But, seeing that Dr. Cone has been so egregiously mistaken in his calculations as to the relation the Pedobaptists would sustain to this movement, let us see if another of the great leaders has not been equally so. Dr. Cone was the President of the American Bible Union. I quote from one of the Vice-Presidents, Mr. A. Campbell, in his address to the Bible Convention at Memphis, Tenn., as published in the Millennial Harbinger for June, 1852. Hear him:

"I am fully of the opinion that those practicing the *immersion* of believers are the only people that can make a really valuable and faithful translation of the New Testament. They have in Protestant Christendom the only commanding and favorable stand-point for such a work. Their eyes are couched. They can see what no man looking through the leather spectacles of Pedobaptism and Pedo-rantism can see in the Christian institution. I speak experiment-

ally as well as theoretically, having been on the top of Mount Sinai before I stood upon the top of Mount Zion. I know the horizon of both these time-honored summits. I therefore silence all cavil as to their incompetency, and strongly declare the conviction that they, and they only, can furnish a version worthy of the age."
"*Pedobaptists and Baptists will never agree to make a new version.* Not one Pedobaptist will touch the ark of our sanctuary, fearing he might be stricken dead. Why should he? How could he? It would be suicidal on his part to raise the tower that would certainly fall upon himself. If an angel in disguise should substitute *immerse* for *baptize*, he would say he came not from the skies. He would not, true to his party, improve the volume in any thing that would crush him in every thing dear to him as a Pedobaptist. Such politicians form no such entangling alliances. While it is a show of generosity or catholicity on our part to invite him, he will, with all complaisance, say, with one of olden time, 'I pray you, sir, have me excused.' None but immersionists

can unite in this work, and none but they could do justice to the subject."

Let the reader compare the above with the language of the "Address for Prayer and Aid," and it will appear that Mr. Campbell has been as much mistaken in his calculations as the President, Dr. Cone.

And what makes the blunder of Mr. Campbell the more remarkable is, that it has been committed very recently—only about two years ago. Mr. Campbell himself, it is believed, is one of the translators. And at the time this language was uttered, some at least of these *leather-spectacled men* were in the employ of the Union as translators. It is very strange that he should not have been aware that he had some of these *blind gentlemen* as his colleagues in making "*a translation worthy of the age.*"

"*Pedobaptists and Baptists will never agree to make a new version,*" says Mr. Campbell. But they have agreed to do so, according to the American Bible Union, through Dr. Cone and others of her advocates. "Not one Pedobaptist will touch the ark of our sanctuary, fearing he might be stricken dead." Yet not *one* but *many*, reckless of the bolt that may strike them "*dead*," are not only *touching* the Baptist ark, according to the advocates of the movement, but have hold of it with both hands, and are, indeed, chiefly concerned in securing for it a destination *in the water*, which its friends so much desire. "Why should he?" asks Mr. Campbell. Why, in order to get *the money*, if for nothing else. "How could he?" he asks again. Why, simply by spurning all the dictates of honor and principle, and submitting to the dictates, not, it is true, of King James or the bishops, but of the American Bible Union. "It would be suicidal on his part to raise the tower that would certainly fall upon himself." And yet Pedobaptists are not only assisting to raise the tower that shall elevate the immersionists, as they fondly hope, into the heaven of ecclesiastical exclusiveness, but they are chiefly concerned in the erection of the tower, though it may fall on them and break their ecclesiastical heads. "If an angel in disguise should substitute *immerse* for *baptize*, he would say he came not from the skies." But he is not going to stand off and await the contingency referred to. He is engaged in helping to put *immerse* for *baptize*. He is not going to wait for an angel to do it. "He would not, true to his party, improve the volume in any thing that would crush him in every thing dear to him as a Pedobaptist." Yet he has engaged in what is claimed to be an effort to improve the volume, at least to make it teach *immersion* for *baptism*, whether it "*crushes him*" in every thing dear to him as a Pedobaptist, or in any thing, or not. It is not likely that those Pedobaptists engaged in this work hold *any thing* that they claim to believe or practice of such worth that they would not be willing to sell it for money. For some reason these Pedobaptists are willing to be *crushed.* "Such politicians form no such entangling alliances." And yet, according to the address, they have formed just such an alliance. "While it is a show of generosity or catholicity on our part to invite him, he will, with all com-

4

plaisance, say, with one of olden time, 'I pray you, sir, have me excused.'" But, according to the address of the Union, there are Pedobaptists who have not asked to be excused. For the sake of the money, they have entered into *"written contract"* to "come up to the help of the Lord against the mighty," in this enterprise.

The hypocritical *"show of generosity or catholicity"* spoken of by Mr. Campbell might have been spared. They might have invited Pedobaptists *candidly* and *sincerely*, had they known they could have been bought for money.

These men, according to Mr. Campbell and the address, have turned traitors, for some consideration deemed by them of more value than the interests of their party; and I suppose it must be the money they get. The love of money was so strong in Judas, that even for the small sum of "thirty pieces of silver" he sold his Master to his enemies. And as human nature, under similar circumstances, is the same in all ages, there are, no doubt, men in Pedobaptist Churches who would be willing to sell the interests of their party for money. And it is no reflection upon Pedobaptist Churches to make this admission.

Mr. Campbell makes the case still stronger. He says: "I am fully of the opinion that those practicing the immersion of believers are the only people that *can* make a really valuable translation. They have . . . the only commanding stand-point for such a work. Their eyes are *couched*. They can see what no man looking through the leather spectacles of Pedobaptism and Pedo-rantism can see in the Christian institution." They have no leather spectacles of any kind on. They can see well enough to do the work. Mr. Campbell speaks not merely from theory, but from experience. He is a man of experience. He knows what he says. He speaks what he does know, and testifies to what he has seen, *i. e.*, since his eyes were "*couched.*" He knows from experience the horizon of both the time-honored summits of Mount Sinai and Mount Zion. He was once on the summit of Mount Sinai, amidst its clouds and darkness, with those same "*leather spectacles*" on. But, fortunately for Mr. Campbell, he long ago descended from that terrible summit, and passed the Jordan, and has now gotten to the summit of Mount Zion, leaving his old *"Pedobaptist and Pedo-rantist* leather spectacles" either in the Jordan, or on the other side. And from his own experience he can testify that none but those who, like himself, have made this transition by passing through "*the Jordan's yielding wave,*" and getting rid of their "*leather spectacles,*" could "do justice to the subject." None but such as stand with Mr. Campbell on the Mount Zion of *Immersion* are free from *ignorance* and *prejudice*. None but the immersionists are *honest* enough to make "*a translation worthy of the age.*" None but they understand the languages in which the Scriptures were originally written sufficiently well.

Well, the question is, how will they get along with these *Pedos*, with *uncouched eyes*, sitting away off yonder on the cold and dark "Mount Sinai in Arabia, which gendereth to bondage," with their "*leather spectacles*" over their eyes, (if they have any,) and yet employed, *under pay*, to assist in doing "a great work?"

The friends of the movement must be, I think, hard put to it to have to pay *such* men to perform a work which they are not capable of performing.

And is it not well known that one of the chief objections to King James's translation is, that it was made by Pedobaptists, and especially Episcopalians—that "there was not one Baptist among the translators?" And now the boast is, that not only are there Pedobaptists among their translators, but that the majority of them are Pedobaptists. It is stated in the "Address for Prayer and Aid," that "more than half the work already done has been performed by scholars not connected with immersionist denominations; and we anticipate that this will hold true until the New Testament is finished."

There must be a great scarcity of learned men among the advocates of the movement, that they have to take men so utterly unsuitable for the work, according to their own showing. There is a question of morals involved which demands some attention. If these Pedobaptist translators are really in favor of the main design of this movement, (and are helping it forward with all their might,) i. e., ultra-immersionists, and yet, at the same time, are identified with Pedobaptist denominations, professing to believe in Pedobaptist doctrines, and conforming to Pedobaptist usages, in what light do they appear in a moral point of view? Professing to be Pedobaptists to the world, and yet secretly engaged in helping to make a translation of the Holy Scriptures, on immersionist and anti-Pedobaptist principles, which shall (as the advocates of the movement contend it will) overturn every principle which they profess to hold sacred, and which, in their vows of ordination, they have most solemnly pledged to vindicate and teach!

But it is said that they are left unrestrained to make such a version as they believe to be legitimate. But, then, will not their work pass in review before a Committee of the Union, constituted for this very purpose? Certainly this is the case, as will be shown in another place. And if the work of these revisors does not come up to the standard of a *faithful* translation, as regards βαπτίζω, or any other word, will they not be bound to make it do so? And so it will not be their work at all which shall be finally endorsed by the American Bible Union, unless they should do it to suit the Union.

But it may be said again, that only those portions of the Scriptures which do not contain the words involving the issue will be assigned to these "*leather-spectacled*" men: that they will not be regarded as competent to translate any thing but Moses and the Prophets; and hardly them. This will not relieve them from moral difficulties. In this case they are chargeable with aiding and abetting a measure whose main design they profess to condemn.

In any view that can be taken of the case of these men, judging from what the advocates of revision have said of them, they are either unprincipled men, willing to sell themselves and their principles for money; or if good men, in their intentions and purposes, they are very defective in their views of moral obligation, and have consequently been misled. In any view that we are able to take of their case, they are not the men to make a version of the Holy Scriptures, to be the rule of the faith and the practice of the Church and the world. Men whose views are so defective, or whose consciences are so elastic, are not the men to be trusted in a matter of so much importance.

And, strange to say, the advocates of this movement trumpet this thing abroad with the highest degree of triumph, as a proof of the non-sectarian character of it, in order that they may gain proselytes, and get prayers offered in their behalf, and secure aid in money to help pay these very worthy and consistent gentlemen for the work they are performing!

But who are the translators? The names of some of them have escaped from the profound secrecy which had enshrouded them; but as to the majority of them, we know nothing. The policy, from the beginning, has been to observe the profoundest secrecy. But who are the trans-

IMMERSIONISTS AGAINST THE BIBLE. 105

lators? What are their names? Where do they reside? Of what congregations have they charge? Or in what institutions of learning are they employed?

Dr. Williams thus refers to this fact:

"And in giving not the names of the translators whom you employ, is it regard to truth or expediency that dictates this remarkable and mysterious reserve? In the preparation of the received version, the names of the learned and orthodox men to be employed were published. The Jews, in their offerings to the Tabernacle, knew as skilful workmen the Bezaleel and Aholiab, who were to form from their gifts the furniture of the sanctuary. When Solomon called from Tyre the highly endowed Hiram to build the temple, do we read that he introduced the architect to the tribes without a name, and wearing a mask? Why repair the goodly edifice of our Scriptures in so covert a manner? You inform us that contracts have been made with some scholars, are about to be made with others, and you ask for funds in their aid and support.

Should we not know the men whom we thus endorse and sustain? When Paul sent men to gather and bear the contributions of the churches, he presented them as well-known and trustworthy —'the messengers of the churches and the glory of Christ.' If funds in almsgiving need known and approved distributors, do not the funds asked for Scripture translation deserve also as much publicity and reliability in the case of men who are to be by these funds sustained in work for the churches? Have we not a right to know whether the men who are to interpret for us God's word, dwell in the tents and speak the dialect of Ashdod, or whether they belong to the tribes and speak the language of Zion? Surely Baptists have not been wont to ask this implicit confidence in the anonymous and unknown."—(Tract No. 10, published by the American Bible Union.)

And just listen to the answer they give to this, in the same tract: "Their names may not be published at present. Could their publication serve any useful or important purpose, without subjecting the persons themselves to the relentless persecution with which all who were known to take any prominent part in the work of revision have been followed, there would be no objection, we presume, to such publicity. But they are engaged in a great work, and would not like to be annoyed by the opponents of revision in a guerilla warfare which has been waged against every man's reputation whom mere rumor represented as having some connection with the Bible Union."

The fear of persecution is given as the apology for this jesuitical course. What! men engaged in so noble a work as this is claimed to be, and not willing to be persecuted for the sake of it?

Is not here a piece of the most consummate priestcraft that was ever attempted to be practiced in a Protestant country? It almost *out-jesuits* Roman *Jesuitism* itself. They deliberately ask for *"prayer and aid"* from Baptists and others, and, at the same time, with the utmost *sang-froid*, refuse to let it be known whom they are to pray for, or to aid by their contributions!

CHAPTER VI.

THE TACTICS OF THE MOVEMENT, CONTINUED.

IN the last two chapters I have exhibited, in part, the tactics of the advocates of this movement, employed to divert the attention of the public from the *main design*. I have quoted from some of their publications a denial, not only that the main object is to substitute *immerse* for *baptize*, but a denial that such a substitution constitutes "any essential or determined part" in the enterprise: that "the Bible Union have never joined issue with their opponents on this point." And, as the reader will recollect, I quoted, from the very same documents, passages in which *this very thing* which they so positively deny is admitted—at least, indirectly. I have aimed all the time to keep before the mind of the reader the main design of the movement, i. e., the putting of *immerse* in the New Testament in the place of *baptize*. And I again repeat, that *this is the main design, unless Drs. Cone and McClay have been totally misled on this subject from the beginning of the movement;* or, if they have not been misled, they have wilfully sought to mislead the public. We have noticed the jesuitical expedient of representing that a large proportion of *the learned men* engaged in the work of translating hold their ecclesiastical connections with Pedobaptist denominations, thereby endeavoring to mislead the public, as we conceive, by making the impression that the forthcoming version is not to be sectarian.

We showed that if the American Bible Union have not abandoned their original purpose, and these Pedobaptist scholars are true to their ecclesiastical connections, they are not the men to be employed in this work : that, admitting that the principles upon which the enterprise was begun are retained, these Pedobaptist learned men are acting dishonestly. And, therefore, so far from the fact of these Pedobaptists being employed in the work of revision being an argument *in favor of it*, it is really one of the strongest arguments that can be used against it. In this chapter I will notice another expedient to hide the main design a little longer. It is this: They have published, and are circulating abroad, parts of the revision of the New Testament, in which neither the word βαπτίζω, nor any of its derivatives, occurs in the original; and they are exhibiting these as proof that the version, when completed, will not be sectarian. One portion of the work commences with the Second Epistle of Peter, and embraces the book of Revelation; the other portion contains the first and second chapters of Matthew. Now, a much more natural arrangement, as far as the first-named portion is concerned, would have been to have commenced with the Epistle of James, and then what are called the General Epistles would have been embraced. At least, it is very unnatural not to have embraced *the First Epistle* of Peter. Why was this left out in this first *specimen* of the new version? Why, simply because *baptisma* occurs in this epistle in the original. And it would not have suited the Jesuitism of the movement to let the main design appear in so prominent a manner at this critical period in its history. They can now exhibit these fragments of the forthcoming version, and say, "See! here is a part of the new version; and you can examine it yourself, and we defy you to detect any thing sectarian in it." This they have done; and many, without reflecting, are misled.

It is said that the first-named portion of the work was performed by one of the eminent Pedobaptist scholars employed in the great work.

This being the fact in the case, this worthy gentleman may have had some conscientious scruples about translating any portion of the New Testament involving the main issue. And, to suit the arrangement to the case of this worthy personage, this part of the work *was laid off* for him. But it admirably suits the purposes of the advocates of the movement in the way I have described. Much capital is sought to be made with it. The dear "*common people,*" for whose benefit the whole movement was professedly set on foot, are sought to be *humbugged;* so that when the whole of the New Testament comes out with *immerse* exalted into the place of *baptize,* they may receive it as the revelation of God. But when the history of the movement is understood, it requires but little *acumen* to see quite through this trick.

In this *specimen* of the new version they could not come out on the main issue, simply because the word involving it is not in the original. But when the whole of the New Testament shall appear in the *new garb, look out! Immerse* and its cognates will be in the place of *baptize* and its cognates. *Immerse* will then "be *printed—* PRINTED IN THE BIBLE," as Dr. Cone says it ought to be. This will be the case, we say, unless the leaders in "the greatest enterprise of the age" should get frightened out of their *long-cherished* purpose, to have their strange dogma of "*dip, and nothing but dip,*" in the New Testament. This may be the case. For not only are the *Pedos* coming "down upon them with tremendous power," but the large majority of their own denomination, and the large majority of their greatest and most learned men, are down on the movement like an *avalanche*, as far as the English Scriptures are concerned. It is only a fragment of the Baptist denomination, and the great body of the Campbellites, that are united in the movement.

They have precedent for backing out. The majority of the American and Foreign Bible Society, though they had formed the purpose of having an immersionist version of the English Scriptures, yet, as we have shown, when the question came to be tested in 1850, they backed out from it. On this account, and no other, as we have shown, the minority seceded, and formed the American Bible Union; and now, possibly, the Union may give up the original and main purpose after all. We shall see.

It may be proper to give additional proof that the portion of the new version which has appeared, furnishes no guaranty that when the whole of it appears it will not be sectarian. There have already appeared two versions of the New Testament under the auspices of the friends of this movement since the Baptists seceded from the American Bible Society, whose character very clearly indicates what the forthcoming version is to be. Large editions of these versions have been printed; and they have been disseminated broadcast in the whole country, and are in the hands of "*the common people,*" for whom they were designed.

In 1838, a version of the New Testament was published by the American and Foreign Bible Society, bearing on the title-page the following imprint: "*New York: Stereotyped by White and Hagar, for the American and Foreign Bible Society. John Gray, Printer,* 1838."

This edition contains *no immersion* in the *text*, but there accompanies it on a fly-leaf a *glossary*, or *dictionary*, giving the *meaning* of seven words which the Society were not willing to risk in the hands of "*the mass of the unlearned,*" without explanation.

Here follows this learned "*fly-leaf*" glossary:

IMMERSIONISTS AGAINST THE BIBLE. 115

"MEANING OF CERTAIN WORDS USED IN THIS VERSION.

Greek.	This version.	Proper meaning.
Angelos,	Angel,	Messenger.
Baptisma,	Baptism,	Immersion.
Baptizo,	Baptize,	Immerse.
Episcopos,	Bishop,	Overseer.
Agape,	Charity,	Love.
Ecclesia,	Church,	Congregation.
Pascha,	Easter,	Passover."

Now, of the explanations given to these seven words, except in the case of *Charity* and *Easter*, they are perfect *nonsense*—at least in many instances. To prove it, let the reader substitute these meanings in the following passages: Heb. ii. 5, 7, 9, 16; xiii. 2 : 1 Cor. vi. 3 : John v. 4 : Luke xx. 36 : Acts xxiii. 8 : 1 Tim. iii. 1–3, etc.

But why are these words arrayed here with *baptism* and *baptize?* Why, *simply* and *mainly* to have an excuse for giving "*the proper meaning*" of *baptism and baptize*. They must pass these terms through the ordeal, in order that, with the greater show of propriety, they might put *baptism* and *baptize* on the *rack*, and torture out of them "*the proper meaning,*" that is, "*dip, and nothing but dip.*"

The other version, published already by the friends of the-revision movement, is that prepared by Messrs. Cone and Wyckoff, and proposed to the American and Foreign Bible Society "for its adoption and circulation," since the publication of the one above named. This version has been scattered through the land in thousands of copies. The glossary expedient is abandoned in this version, and *immerse* and *immersion* are "*printed*—PRINTED IN THE BIBLE," as Dr. Cone (who was chiefly concerned in preparing it) contends it ought to be. Here is a step further in "the greatest enterprise of the age." *Baptize* and *baptism* are turned out of the Bible, and the darling idea of "*dip, and nothing but dip,*" which is to open the eyes of the world and make them *immersionists*, is put in its stead. But what becomes of the words that accompanied *baptism* and *baptize* in the "*fly-leaf*" edition? Why, "*the proper meaning*" of only three of them (*viz.*, Charity, Bishop, and Easter) is given, and Angel and Church are left as in our version. Hear Dr. A. Newton on this subject, in the *True Baptist*: "How is this? The same men, the President and Secretary of the same Society, first give us a New Testament with "*a glossary*" in which the reader is warned against the improper and false renderings of certain words in the text, and 'the proper meaning' is given to secure him from being led astray by these false renderings; and yet, when they come to make a version just as they would have it themselves, they do not give us 'the proper meaning,' but still retain that which they had thus solemnly pronounced improper and false. How is this? Was it an oversight?

"But as to *baptize* and *baptism*, they are by no means so forgetful. They make sure of these. These are uniformly given in their 'proper meaning.' Amidst 'several hundred emendations' which they say they have made in this edition, the *angels* and the *churches* are left to stand undisturbed in their old places in the Bible. *Baptism* and *baptize*, however, are rigidly excluded, and nowhere in this version are permitted to have place. In their stead, we have *immersion, immerse*—modal terms, unsuited to express the intent of the original, and directly in conflict with the act enjoined in God's word."

I quote the following from the manifesto accompanying the issue of this version: "In addition to such specific cases of the direct perversion of the word of God in support of the dogmas and usages of the Church of England, it may be remarked that obscurity and indefiniteness are thrown over the ordinance of *baptism*, in order to shield from the condemnation of holy writ, the sprinkling and pouring substituted for *immersion* in the practices of that Church. The term *baptizo* and its cognates, which, if correctly translated, would enjoin *immersion*, are not, when referring to the ordinance, translated, but transferred from the original Greek with Anglicised terminations."—(" Bible Translated," in New York Chronicle, p. 49.) I will give a few specimens from this version, that the reader may see what improvement they have made in favor of their peculiar dogma. Here they are:

Matt. iii. 11 : " I indeed immerse you in water unto repentance; but he that cometh after me is mightier than I, whose shoes I am not worthy to bear: he will *immerse* you in the Holy Spirit and fire."

John i. 25–28 : "And they asked him, Why immersest thou then," etc. " John answered them, saying, I immerse in water," etc. " These things were done in Bethabara, beyond Jordan, where John was immersing. And I knew him not; but he that sent me to immerse in water," etc., " the same is he that immerseth in the Holy Spirit."

Mark vii. 4 : "And when they come from market, except they immerse, they eat not. And many other things there are which they have received to hold, as the immersing of cups, and pots, and brazen vessels, and couches."

Luke xi. 38 : "When the Pharisee saw it, he marvelled that he had not first immersed before dinner."

Mark x. 38, 39 : "Can ye drink of the cup that I drink of? and be immersed with the immersion that I am immersed with? Ye shall indeed drink of the cup that I drink of; and with the immersion that I am immersed with ye shall be immersed."

Rom. vi. 3, 4 : "Know ye not that so many of us as were immersed into Jesus Christ, were immersed into his death? Therefore we are buried with him by immersion unto death," etc.

Acts i. 5 : "For John indeed immersed in water; but ye shall be immersed in the Holy Spirit not many days hence."

Acts xi. 15, 16 : "And as I began to speak, the Holy Spirit fell on them as on us at the beginning. Then remembered I the word of the Lord, how he said, John immersed in water, but ye shall be immersed in the Holy Spirit."

Now let the reader bear in mind that these two versions were published and have been circulated by the advocates of the revision movement. It is true they were published by the American and Foreign Bible Society; but it was previously to their abandoning the idea of a new version in English. And note, that they were gotten up principally through the influence of Messrs. Cone and Wyckoff, who went off at the head of the secession in 1850. And the latter edition of the above two has been and is being diligently circulated by the agents of the Union. They have, therefore, fully endorsed it.

And from these versions, does it not appear very clearly what they are after? These versions were put forth and sent abroad as *harbingers* or forerunners of the denominational version. They are intended to be the means, in part, of preparing the way for it.

I have quoted from the friends of the movement, showing what they thought *should be* the version which is sought. In these versions there appears what they have actually done, as demonstrating what kind of a version they are determined to make it.

In the former of these *preparatory versions* they put immerse, etc., in the *glossary* on the "*fly-leaf*" In the latter they exclude *baptize*, etc., from the text, and put *immerse*, etc., in their place.

They are, therefore, committed to this feature in the new version, beyond all possibility of getting out of it, unless, indeed, they give up the whole enterprise as a magnificent failure.

CHAPTER VII.

DISPARAGEMENT OF THE COMMON VERSION.

In this chapter I will notice some of the charges brought against King James and the translators of the common version, and especially against the version itself.

These charges are made for the purpose, of course, of destroying confidence in the common version, so as to make way for their own one-sided, sectarian translation.

I will only present a few of the many charges they have made, as an indication of the *animus* of the movement.

The English Bible is spoken of as "Scriptures in the dress and mask an arbitrary monarch of Popish extraction, of Presbyterian education, but defender of the faith of Episcopacy, chose to give them."

"Was made to suit other denominations."

That "it perpetuates ignorance by concealment, and error by misinterpretation, on the point at which we are at issue," (*i. e.*, of course, baptism.)

Again: "The fact is, instead of performing the work to the best of their knowledge and skill, they (the translators) were obliged to submit themselves, as passive instruments, to the dictation of a monarch noted for passion, pedantry, and self-will."

· Again: "The evils which have accrued from the introduction of a single word imposed by foreign influence, and the bigotry of an earthly prince, no human mind can compute."

Again: "One of the important ordinances of the gospel, described by the Holy Spirit as with a sunbeam, has been covered up and hid from the great mass of the people by *the popish artifice of transfer.*"

"Under the class of old ecclesiastical words, baptize was included, and, therefore, the translators did not feel themselves at liberty *to translate* it, but merely gave it *an English termination.*"

"But the King, it should seem, did not wish the meaning of the word to be known: our translators acquiesce, and so they wrap it up."

"Baptists surely will not cleave to the fascinating Latin Vulgate *Baptizare*, 'chipped,' as Stovel says, 'to suit the Saxon taste, as given by the word baptize, *crawling like a lizard from a papal swamp.*'"

In a discussion of Revision, as reported in the New York Chronicle, the Rev. Mr. Grafton said: "I have heard that a remark was made here last night, which, had I been here, I should have feared God would have sent a flash of lightning to avenge. I heard that his holy word was compared to a *blind, dumb dog.*"

Mr. S. W. Cone: "I protest that it was not the case."

Rev. Dr. Dowling: "I understood that you meant that we ministers had been all our lives palming *a lame dog for a sheep.*"

Mr. S. W. Cone: "I said that every Baptist minister had been attempting, through the whole course of his ministry, to prove that *baptize* means *to immerse;* and I said that the word *baptize* was a *lame dog.*"

Rev. Mr. Kingsford: "I feel constrained to say that I did not understand the gentleman so."

It will be observed that Mr. Cone does not make the case any better after all.

Let the reader particularly notice the epithets applied to the English Bible, to King James, and the translators. And these extracts, perhaps, do not contain a fair specimen of the abuse they have used. They fall, perhaps, much below the spirit that has been manifested in this regard in some of the publications of the friends of the movement, and in addresses before the people. In a neighboring village, not long ago, the ablest advocate of revision, perhaps, in the West, in an address upon the subject, pointed to the common version with supreme contempt, and denounced it as containing *falsehood.*

Another advocate of the movement, in an adjoining county to this, most solemnly declared that if he were on his dying-bed, he could not call his child to his bedside and put the common version in his hand and tell him that it would safely guide him to heaven. What effect must such attacks upon the word of God have, made by men professing godliness!*

---

* In the appeal of Messrs. Cone and Wyckoff, published in the New York Chronicle for 1850, pp. 55–75, the following language is used: "We hesitate not to say, that if any other book of the size, disfigured by half the number of faults of a similar description, were proposed as a reading-book in any district school in this State, (New York,) to form the taste of youth in the use of correct English, it would be rejected by the school committee with disdain."

Says Dr. Williams, in his letter to the Amity Street Church, as contained in a pamphlet entitled, "The Common English Version,"—"Against the received version in its present state have been alleged, in language of great directness and ruggedness, faults in grammar and style that would banish any other book from our common schools; and errors in translation, 'obvious errors,' that endanger 'every schoolboy,' 'as he becomes familiar with the Greek Testament;' so that *no care on the part of a teacher can prevent a germ of infidelity from taking root in his breast,* when he sees that Christians, while professing the most ardent love for the truth, prefer to circulate *the most palpable falsehoods* under the name of God's revealed word, rather than correct them when in their power.'

One thing, however, is very clear from the above quotations; and that is, that if *immerse* had been put in the place of *baptize*, King James and the translators would not have been regarded as so great sinners. That they did not do this, is the burden of the complaint. If "*dip, and nothing but dip,*" had been where they think it ought to be, they would be content. Thus, Mr. Cushman, as already quoted: "It (the English Bible) is not sufficiently defective, except in regard to *baptism* and Church order, to be dis-

---

"The authors of the version are impeached as having used needlessly and unwarrantably '*a most irreverent oath;*' and as having 'put it into the apostle's mouth;' of having, with express design, clouded the sense of Scripture, '*in order the more effectually to obscure the perceptions of an ordinary reader* in regard to the true nature of the ordinance,' (baptism,) and to force upon the mind 'a certain erroneous conviction, almost uniformly mistranslated a certain preposition;' and, finally, with having used, and that often, to describe the third person in the adorable Trinity, 'a term of absurdity and impropriety,' and even '*manifest blasphemy.*'"

In reading such abuse as the above, one almost imagines himself reading some of the lowest and most profane of Voltaire and Paine's attacks on the Bible.

trusted as a guide to truth and duty." The impression is sought to be made, as in the above extracts, that King James originated the idea of the common version; that it was secured by his influence as the sovereign of Great Britain; and that its adoption by the people of his realm was the result of the enforcement of the royal authority. No account of the whole matter could be farther from the truth, as I will show from the most unquestionable authority.

I have before me "Annals of the English Bible, by Christopher Anderson, of Edinburgh, abridged and continued by S. I. Prime." Mr. Anderson, I learn, is a member of the Baptist Church in Scotland, a gentleman evidently of learning, and who gives evidence in this work of very laborious and diligent research. His work is a standard, so far as the history of the English Scriptures is concerned, and his testimony ought not to be objected to by the advocates of the new version movement, as he is a Baptist of very high standing.

The main object of Mr. Anderson in this work

is to show that, from Wycliffe's translation of the Holy Scriptures from the Latin Vulgate, and Tyndale's version from the Hebrew and Greek, into our language, to the present time, the work has been carried forward, not only *without the aid or countenance* of ecclesiastical or civil authority or power, but *in despite of both.* And no one can fail to see, who reads the work, that he has fully made out what he proposes.

And what does Mr. Anderson say in regard to the part which King James had in the common version? I quote from Book III., section iv., pp. 400–403.

"Up to the present moment, (A. D. 1604,) the history of the English Bible had maintained a character peculiar to itself. Originating with no mere patron, whether royal or noble, the undertaking had never yet been promoted at the personal expense of any such party. But now, in regard to that version of the sacred volume, which for two hundred and thirty years has been read with delight, from generation to generation, and proved the effectual means of knowledge, holiness, and joy to millions, it may be imagined by some, as there was another and a final change, that our history must at last change, or, in other words, *forfeit its character.* If, however, the accounts frequently given of our present version have been involved in as much inaccuracy of statement as they have been with regard to all the preceding changes, there is the greater necessity for the public mind being disabused; and that, too, whether in Britain or America, or the British foreign dependencies. This is a subject which alike concerns them all, as they all read and prize the same version.

"If because that a dedication to James the First of England has been prefixed to many copies, though not to many others; and if because not only historians, at their desks, but lawyers at the bar, and even judges on the bench, have made most singular mistakes, it has therefore been imagined by any, or many, that the present version of our Bible was either suggested by this monarch, or that he was at any personal expense in the undertaking; or that he ever issued a single line of authority, by way of proclamation, with respect to it; it is more than time that the delusion should come to an end. The original and authentic documents of the time are so far explicit, that just in proportion as they are sifted, and the actual circumstances placed in view, precisely the same independence of royal bounty, and, on the part of the people at large, the same superiority to all royal dictation, which we have beheld all along, will become apparent. James himself, however vain, is certainly not so much to be blamed for any different impression, as some others who have misrepresented his Majesty. On the other hand, his character was such, that to many writers it has occasioned some exercise of patience even to refer to it. But since his name occurs in connection with this final revision of the English Bible, it is of the more importance to ascertain the exact amount of this connection. From the moment in which he was invited to the throne, and to be king of Great

Britain, his own favorite term, down to the year in which our present version was published, his 'royal progress' is forced upon our notice.

"Elizabeth had expired on the 24th of March, 1603, when the King of Scotland succeeded as James the First, finally assuming the style of King of Great Britain, France, and Ireland. Having left Edinburgh for England, on Tuesday the 5th of April, James proceeded, by the way of Berwick and Newcastle, through York to London, where he did not arrive till the 7th of May. Throughout this journey he had already furnished a strong contrast, in point of character, to his predecessor. With regard to rewards, whether in point of honor or emolument, Elizabeth had been so sparing that she had been charged with avarice. But James having once procured from London such supplies as might enable him to advance in befitting style, actually hunted most of the way, scattering the honors of knighthood with such profusion along the road, that by the day he entered his capital the number of his knights was about one hundred and fifty; and before one fortnight had passed, or by the 20th of May, 'they were accounted at two hundred and thirty-seven, or better, since the time he entered Berwick,' on the 6th of April. The queen, with her children, having followed in June, the coronation took place in July; after which, his Majesty immediately returned, with great ardor, to his favorite sport of hunting. Though now entered into his thirty-ninth year, and having affairs to manage which had demanded all the talents of an Elizabeth, never was a boy let loose from school more bent upon his amusement.

"Of the learning or talent to be found in England, where he had done little else than follow the hounds and the hares, James as yet could know next to nothing. Of Oxford and Cambridge he was equally ignorant. He had not called any circle of learned men around him, nor, indeed, ever did. Such also was the state of his finances, when necessity forced him to call a parliament. 'It was,' says Sir James McIntosh, 'his last resource. He had exhausted his credit with the money-dealers, both in London and Holland, to supply his prodigalities, before he issued his proclamation for the meeting of parliament, on the 19th of March.'

"It was in the midst of his sport at Wilton, and his preparations for the arraignment of Sir Walter Raleigh, that James issued a proclamation, dated the 24th day of October, 'Touching a meeting for the hearing and for the determining things pretended to be amiss in the Church.' This meeting, known ever since as '*the Conference at Hampton Court*,' was held in the drawing-room there, on Saturday, Monday, and Wednesday, the 14th, 16th, and 18th of January, 1604.

"The Conference, it will be understood, was not with *any official body* of men whatever; and it should also be remembered, that however exalted were the ideas of James himself, as to his prerogatives, or of his right and title to the throne, strictly speaking, or according to law, he was *not yet king of England;* nor could he be till the assembling of Parliament. That was the point to which, as we have seen, Lord Cecil was looking forward. This was a conference, therefore, of the king by courtesy, for the time being, with only nine bishops, eight deans, an archdeacon, two professors of divinity from Oxford, two from Cambridge, to which one native of Scotland, Mr. Patrick Galloway, formerly of Perth, was also admitted. Nor were even all these parties present on any one day.

"The 16th of January was the time appointed for hearing of things 'pretended to be amiss,' as the proclamation had phrased it; and it was among them that the necessity for another revision or translation of the Bible was first mentioned.

"Dr. John Rainolds, a man of high and unblemished character, then in his 55th year, was at that time nearly, if not altogether, the most eminent individual for learning and erudition in the kingdom. He was now the President of Corpus Christi College, and the chief speaker on this occasion. . . . .

"As presented by Rainolds was the following: 'That a translation be made of the whole Bible, *as consonant as can be to the original Hebrew and Greek*, and this to be set out and printed, *without any marginal notes*, and only to be used in all churches of England in time of Divine service.' Now by this version of the story the exclusion of all marginal *notes* ORIGINATED with Rainolds, as well as the proposal of a new translation.

"The first Parliament held by the King assembled on the 19th of March, 1604, and the Convocation on the following day. The Primate, Whitgift, having expired on the 29th of February, Bancroft, the Bishop of London, was appointed to preside. James had commenced these proceedings with a speech longer than many a sermon; but at last, not being in the best humor with his English Parliament, he dissolved it on the 7th of July, and the Convocation rose.

"Among all the business of either house, not one word was spoken then respecting the Scriptures; nor do we hear of any movement in consequence of what had passed at Hampton Court, till the end of June. Some time had been required for the selection of suitable scholars, and before the end of that month a list was presented to James for his acceptance. They had been selected for him, and he of course approved."

Now, in the light of the above, what becomes of the allegation that the common version was secured at the instance of James to subserve his purposes as an individual and a sovereign? For it appears, 1, that at the time of the session of the Hampton Court Conference, James was not, according to law, *King of England at all*, nor was he till more than two months afterwards. Consequently, the Conference itself was vested with no civil or ecclesiastical authority. It was composed of "no official body of men whatever." The King was present, and presided by courtesy, and not officially. It appears, 2, that the King was not the mover of the proposition to have a new version. Dr. Rainolds made the motion. He only consented or approved of the measure. It appears, 3, that the King did not even select the translators. They were selected by another, and he only accepted the selection. We learn, 4, that James did not even contribute one cent toward defraying the expenses of the translation, nor of its publication, as we learn from the following extract of a letter sent from the King to all the bishops, by Bancroft, acting as the Archbishop of Canterbury. This is found on page 404 of the work above named:

"Right-trusty and well-beloved brother, we greet you well. Whereas we have appointed certain learned men to the number of four-and-fifty, for the translating of the Bible, and that in this number *diverse* of them either have no ecclesiastical preferment at all, or else so very small as the same is far unmeet for men of their deserts, *and* yet, we of OURSELF *in any convenient time cannot well remedy it:* Therefore, we do hereby require you, that presently you write, in our name, as well to the Bishop of *York*, as to the rest of the bishops of the province of *Canterbury*, signifying unto them that we do will, and straitly charge every one of them, as also the other bishops of the province of York, as they tender our good favor toward them, that (all excuses set apart) when any prebend or parsonage, being rated in our book of taxations, the prebend to twenty pounds at least, and the parsonage to the like sum and upwards, shall next upon any occasion happen to be void, and to be either of their patronage, or of the patronage and gift *of any person whatever*, they do make stay thereof, and admit none unto it, until certifying us of the avoidance of it, and of the name of the patron, if it be not of their own gift, that we may commend for the same some such of the learned men as we shall think fit to be preferred unto it; not doubting of the bishops' readiness to satisfy us herein, or that any of the laity, when we shall in time move them to so good and religious an act, will be unwilling to give us the like due contentment and satisfaction; we ourselves having taken the same order for such prebends and benefices as shall be void in our gift.'

Mr. Anderson says, p. 410, "The first revision of the sacred text by the forty-seven occupied about *four years;* the second examination by twelve, or two selected out of each company, *nine months* more, and the sheets passing through the press other two years, when the Bible of 1611 was finished, and first issued."

We have seen how the first revision was paid for. Let us see how the second, or that by the twelve, was paid for. The historian will tell us on the same page how it was likely done: "Twelve men paid at the rate of thirty shillings each was equal to £18 weekly, and for the thirty-nine weeks £702 must have been expended, which expense was probably borne by Barker, who had the *patent* for printing the Bible.

"The honor of payment for the whole concern, so often ascribed to James the First, is by no means to be taken from him, if one shred of positive evidence can be produced; but this, it is presumed, lies beyond the possibility of research. In this case, therefore, to speak correctly, we have come at last, *not* to an affair of government, *not* to a royal undertaking *at his Majesty's expense*, according to the popular and very erroneous historical fiction, *but simply to a transaction in the course of business.* If we inquire for any single royal grant, or look for any act of personal generosity, we search in vain."—We learn by an additional extract from this work, (pp. 410, 411,) that it was not by the authority of King James, or any power civil or ecclesiastical, that the common version came to be received as the standard version in England, Scotland, and Ireland. "There is one other inquiry to be made, and this, to some minds, may be not the least important. It is this: By whose *influence or authority* was it, that our version of the sacred volume came to be read, not in England alone, but in Scotland and Ireland? This, too, is a question the more interesting to millions, as it is now the Bible of so many distant climes—read not only in America and Canada, but in all the widespread and daily extending British colonies. The reigning king had indeed signified his approbation of the undertaking, and when the Bible was published it bore on its title-page that the version had been 'newly translated out of the original tongues, and with the former translations diligently compared and revised, by his Majesty's special commandment.' In a separate line below, and by itself, we have these words : 'Appointed to be read in churches.' Now, as the book never was submitted to Parliament, never to any Convocation, nor, as far as is known, ever to the Privy Council, James, by this title-page, was simply following or made to follow in the train of certain previous editions. As for Elizabeth, his immediate predecessor, we have already seen that under her long reign there was another revision besides the bishops', and that the former enjoyed the decided preference in public favor; so, in the present instance, that there might be no mistake or misapprehension in regard to the influence of *authority* by which our present Bible came to be universally received, a result somewhat similar took place.

"Thus, for seven or eight years after the present version was published, we find Barker, or Norton and Bill, still printing the Geneva Bible, in ten editions, besides four of the New Testament separately. The fact is, that the royal patentee went on to print both versions to the year 1617, or 1618. After that the Geneva Bibles, so frequently printed in Holland, were imported and sold, without the shadow of inhibition, during the entire reign of James the First, and longer still. As for Scotland, from whence the king had come, that Bible continued to be as much used there as the present version, for more than twenty years after James was in his grave. The influence or authority of James, therefore, cannot once be mentioned when accounting for the final result.

"The Bible was, indeed, first published in 1611, and was still further corrected in 1613; but did James, as a king, take one step to enforce its perusal? Not one: a fact so much the more notable when the overweening conceit of that monarch, and the high terms in which he so frequently expressed himself as to his prerogative, are remembered.

"'We can assign,' says one of the best living authorities in the kingdom, 'we can assign no *authority* for using the present version of the Bible, except that of the Conference at Hampton Court.' But that Conference has been already described; and in the circumstances, it actually amounted to no authority at all in point of a law.

James was not then King of England: though had it been otherwise, that Conference certainly had not the slightest influence in recommending the version to which it gave rise. However, immediately after his Majesty had been recognized by the Parliament, he had spoken *once*, as we have heard; and his solitary letter we have given at length. It was, in part, abortive; and after that, it seems, he must speak *no more;* a circumstance the more worthy of notice, as James was notoriously so fond of speaking officially, and especially by proclamations. In the first nine months of his reign he had issued at least a round dozen; but here there was nothing of the kind. 'After this translation was published,' says one writer, 'the others all dropped off by *degrees*,' that is, in about forty years, 'and this took the place of all, though I do not find that there was any *canon, proclamation, or act of Parliament* to enforce the use of it.'"

This shows the utter baselessness of the assumption, upon the part of advocates of the revision movement of our day, as to the part which was taken by King James in the procurement and circulation of the common version. Ignorance of the history of facts, or blindness caused by an overheated zeal to sustain the interests of a party reckless of the testimony of history, can alone account for the representations and charges which have been made in the premises. I quote the following from the address of Mr. A. Campbell to the Bible Convention at Memphis, April, 1852, as fully agreeing with the facts above quoted:

" But it [the English Bible] originated not with and proceeded not from them [King James and his party]. *It was individual piety, learning, zeal, enterprise, that gave to us our present English Bible.*"

But admitting that King James exercised royal authority in procuring the version in common use, (and we have proved that he did not,) what ground is there for the charge that he left the translators no discretion in the work of translating; that, instead of leaving them to do the work to the best of their knowledge and skill,

IMMERSIONISTS AGAINST THE BIBLE. 147

they "were obliged to yield themselves as passive instruments to the dictates of a monarch?" etc.

This, certainly, is a grave charge; and there ought to have been most satisfactory proof of the justness of it before it was made. But I think I will make it appear to every candid mind that it is an utterly gratuitous and reckless slander.

It is very evident, if King James did exercise the arbitrary power ascribed to him, it will appear in the rules laid down for the direction of the translators. If it does not appear in these, it is evident that its source is in the imaginations of revisionists.

I will quote, as relating to this subject, the 1st, 3d, and 14th rules:

1st. "The ordinary Bible read in the Church, commonly called the Bishops' Bible, to be followed, and as little altered as the original will permit."

3d. "The old ecclesiastical words to be kept; as the word CHURCH, not to be translated CONGREGATION, etc."

14th. "These translations to be used when

they agree better with the text than the Bishops' Bible, viz.: 1. Tyndale's; 2. Matthew's; 3. Coverdale's; 4. Whitchurch's; (*i.e.*, Cranmer's;) 5. The Geneva."

Now, what "*dictation*" is here to be objected to? The Bishops' Bible is to be followed, and as little altered "*as the original will permit.*" (Rule 1st.) Therefore, the original is the ultimate standard recognized. And the translators are left to their free and unrestrained judgment in determining its meaning. Was not this discretion enough? Was this fettering the translators? In addition (Rule 14th) they are left free to follow any or all of five other versions, when they agree better with the text (*i. e.* the original) than the Bishops' Bible. The translators, then, are allowed to make the original Hebrew and Greek their standard: whatever respect they were to pay to the Bishops' Bible, or any other version, they were required, as a *sine qua non*, to conform to the import of the original. This was the ultimate and final standard. The only dictation which appears is, that the original was made the standard of authority in translating. Is this objectionable?

The chief stress, however, is laid upon the third rule. It is charged that under this rule he meant to prohibit the translation of *baptizo*, and some other words, in order to make it "suit other denominations," especially the Episcopalians: that under the restraint of this rule "ignorance is perpetuated by concealment, and error by misinterpretation:" that *baptize* "was imposed by foreign influence and the bigotry of an earthly prince:" that "one of the ordinances of the gospel has been covered up by *the popish artifice of transfer:*" that "the king did not wish the meaning of the word to appear; the translators acquiesce, and so 'they wrap it up:'" *baptizo* being "included in the class of old ecclesiastical words, the translators did not feel themselves at liberty to translate it, but gave it *an English termination.*"

Now, how do these slanderers know that the translators did not feel themselves at liberty to translate *baptizo*, and on this account did not put immerse, or a word of such import, in the place of it?

But let us see if there is any ground for the charge that the third rule restrained and fettered the translators in regard to *baptizo*.

1. We most solemnly deny that the third rule prohibits the translation from the original of *baptizo*, or any other word. It only requires that the old ecclesiastical words be retained, or "*kept.*" The word "*Church*" is the only example given to illustrate the meaning of the rule. But there is no prohibition of the translation of that. That is itself a translation of the original word, *ecclesia*. The original word was not absolutely forbidden to be translated. The only thing absolutely prohibited is that "*congregation*" should be translated from the original, *instead of* "*Church.*" That is all. There is, therefore, no absolute prohibition of translation from the original in this rule at all. And it is only by a most astonishing perversion of its meaning that such a construction can be given to it.

2. But we will suppose, for the sake of argument, that the rule does prohibit the translation

of "old ecclesiastical words" from the original; yet how is it made out that *Baptizo* is one of these, and, therefore, was retained by virtue of the authority of the rule? *Baptize* is not once named in the rule; and yet revisionists speak as confidently upon this subject as if the word were positively named in the rule. It is not there. They "*foist it in.*" They pervert the meaning of the rule, and then apply it to this word. They say, "The king did not wish the meaning of the word to appear." How do they find this out? Not in the rules. They invent this assumption to serve "the greatest enterprise of the age." "The translators acquiesce, and so they wrap it up." Where is the authority for this dark slander? Not in the rules. The purpose is settled to turn *baptize* out of the Bible; and the point is, to secure something as an apology for it, and they can imagine facts when they do not exist.

But, 3. A proof that the translators did not understand the third rule as prohibiting the translation of *baptizo* and its cognates, is found in the fact that *they did translate baptizo.* What, then, becomes of the construction given to the third rule, and of the charge, that the translators were mere "*passive instruments*" in a plan "*to wrap up*" God's holy word?

In Mark vii. 4, two of the derivatives of *baptizo* are found, viz., βαπτίσωνται, *baptisontai*, and βαπτισμοὺς, *baptismous.* In our translation the former is rendered "*wash*," and the latter "*washing.*"

In Heb. ix. 10, βαπτισμοῖς, *baptismois*, is found. It is rendered by "*washings.*"

Now, if the translators were the sycophantic, unprincipled men they are represented as having been, and King James exercised the despotic dictation over them he is said to have done, how are we to account for the fact that the translators did, in three instances at least, translate *baptizo* by a word familiar to "the common people?" This cannot be answered on the ground assumed, that the third rule was understood as prohibiting the translation of *baptizo*, but as requiring its transfer. In these instances we find the translators flying in the face of the king's authority; and, strange to say, we hear of no complaint upon his part, or from any other source.

But, finally, I assume that the translators of the common version, in rendering *baptizo* by *baptize*, did really translate a *Greek* word by an *English* word. At the time our translation was made, *baptize* was as really an English word as it is now. It is true it was taken from the Greek language; but it had been a part and parcel of the English vocabulary for centuries. There was no such thing, then, as tranfer in the use of this word at the time our translation was made. Can the advocates of this movement be ignorant of the fact that words from foreign languages make up a large proportion of the English vocabulary, and that they are just as really entitled to be regarded English words as any other? To show that my position in regard to the history of *baptize* as an English word is correct, I will quote from eminent Baptist ministers, of learning and talents.

Dr. John Dowling, in a tract containing ten

reasons for his opposition to the new version movement, gives as the fourth: "Because the word *baptize is itself, to all intents and purposes, an English word.*"

The Rev. Dr. Ide says: "I suppose that *baptize* is the only English word by which you can translate *baptizo.*"

"It is eight hundred years older, as a native English citizen, than *immerse.*"

The Rev. Dr. Williams says: "On the score of age, the word *baptize* is probably some six centuries older, as an English word, than the term *immerse*, proposed to replace it. Its rights in the English language are older than Magna Charta—older than the Norman conquest—coeval with the very birth of the language properly so called. And yet it is proposed by some to repudiate and reject it as an alien in our dialect."

"Now, where and what are the mighty objections to these rules, [King James's rules to the translators,] which could be suggested to an intelligent and impartial reader? Where are the *manacles* and *fetters*, the *arbitrary dictation*, and the odious despotism? Where are the *masking, mutilation, concealment, and disguise, and wrapping up in obscurity?* Where is the evidence of 'unlawful interference,' 'infringing the liberty of conscience, and laying violent hands on the truth itself?' Where is the proof that the translators were compelled, by royal mandate, to adopt the popish artifice of transfer, and that 'that word which he (Christ) used in the great commission to denote his own initiatory ordinance, was, by order of King James, transferred into our English Bibles?' Where is the evidence that the translators, 'instead of performing the work to the best of their knowledge and skill, were obliged to submit themselves as passive instruments to the dictation of a monarch noted for passion, pedantry, and self-will?'

"There is no evidence of any such thing. The charges are false, whether made through 'ignorance or dishonesty.' I fearlessly avow my conviction of the wisdom, judiciousness, and general liberality of these rules."—(True Baptist, by Dr. A. Newton.)

"With the views which the advocates of this measure entertain of the moral character of the translators of our version, I cannot see how they can have any confidence in any part of it. To be consistent, they should throw it aside as *an unholy thing*. If, as they say, 'the king did not wish the meaning of *baptizo* to appear;' that the translators acquiesce, and so 'they wrap it up,' what must be the inevitable effect of such an imputation upon those who have the slightest suspicion of the possibility of its truth? There never was a mind formed, which, having taken this step, could avoid at once, and certainly, taking the next, and utterly surrendering all confidence in any portion of the translation. All philosophy teaches, universal observation proves, and our Saviour himself declares: 'He that is faithful in that which is least, is faithful also in much; and he that is unjust in the least, is unjust also in much.' If the king did not wish the meaning of one word to be known, and the translators acquiesced, and they wrapped it up in obscurity, in order to conceal its true meaning from the people, no man who is not himself of a base and corrupt heart can have the least degree of respect for them, or for any part of their work, from the beginning of Genesis to the end of Revelation. If I believed the tenth part of the imputations here made by 'the only people' against the forty-seven translators, I should scorn to have their work on my table.

"The charge against them is infinitely worse than the charge of theft, perjury, piracy, or murder. With such men I would scorn to shake hands in open daylight. I should fear to meet such men in the darkness. If I believed they had so little conscience as to conceal any one word in their translation, I should, if it were the last act of my life, consign to the flames every leaf of the Bibles about my house, and leave it solemnly in charge to my children to avoid them as they would the viper's poisonous fang.

"Do 'the only people' believe these charges which they make themselves? I am amazed at their patience and forbearance. I marvel that, standing up before the world as the ministers of heaven to their dying fellow-men, and professing to proclaim the unsearchable riches of Christ, and the way of truth and holiness, as the way to happiness and heaven, they can pollute their clean hands by the touch of this foul, filthy thing, '*crawling like a lizard from a papal swamp.*' How can they excuse themselves for having held up this volume before their congregations for a hundred years, as a light to their feet, and a lamp to their pathway, from this dark world of sin, of sorrow, and of death, to the bright world of light, life, and glory on high? Were they not afraid of the *fearful plagues* written in this book? If the translators slavishly submitted to the manacles and fetters of an arbitrary despot, and, recreant to their high and infinite obligations to God and his truth, sold their consciences for a mess of pottage, doled out to them by a wicked king; or, in base cowardice, and with corrupt purpose, abstracted a single scruple from God's perfect word, or added a pennyweight to its sacred teachings, they deserve the united and endless execrations of all mankind."—*Ibid.*

CHAPTER VIII.

THE IMMERSIONISTS HAVE DONE AND ARE DOING WHAT THEY CHARGE KING JAMES WITH DOING.

In the previous chapter, I think it has been satisfactorily shown that the charges against King James and the translators are utterly groundless: that the translators were left to as wide a discretion as could with reason be desired; that the only absolute restriction laid upon them, as regards translation, was, that they should give the sense of the original Hebrew and Greek. And certainly this cannot be objected to.

In this chapter I think I will make it appear to every candid reader that the sin which the advocates of this movement are charging upon King James, they are guilty of themselves. And it is in accordance with general observation that those who are so reckless in their charges of wrong-doing on others, are likely to be guilty of the same sin, or something worse. Paul has reference to this when he says, in "the old-fashioned Bible," "Therefore thou art inexcusable, O man, whosoever thou art, that judgest; for wherein thou judgest another thou condemnest thyself; for thou that judgest doest the same things."

That the American and Foreign Bible Society, the Bible Translation Society of Great Britain, and the American Bible Union, have in view, as a *sine quâ non* in the versions they are aiming to secure and circulate, that they shall contain words signifying *immerse* in the place of *baptize*, is fully established by the history of the movement, as already presented.

Why did the Asiatic and European Baptists withdraw from the Calcutta and British and Foreign Bible Societies? Why, simply because these Societies would not consent to give money, contributed mainly by Pedobaptists, to aid in the publication of *immersionist* versions of the Holy

Scriptures. And when they had seceded for the sake of this principle, is it likely they would abandon it afterwards? Nay, verily! And accordingly, as has been already shown, when the Bible Translation Society of Great Britain was organized, the second article of their constitution set forth the fact that they would patronize none but *immersionist* versions of the Holy Scriptures. There can be no doubt, then, as to the position of the English Baptists. They leave their translators no alternative in the translation of the words relating to the ordinance of *baptism*. They put the "*manacles*" on in good earnest. If they should patronize any other kind of versions, they would violate their constitution. And will they do this?

Why did the Baptists and other immersionists secede from the American Bible Society in 1835? Simply, as the reader will remember, because that Society would not appropriate its funds, in violation of the great principle on which the Society was organized, to sustain *immersionist* versions of the Holy Scriptures.

Would they have seceded from the Society had it not been for their devotion to *immersion*? Do they complain of any thing else but that the American Bible Society would not permit *baptizo* to be translated? Would it not now be very strange and inconsistent for them, in view of these facts, to think of any thing short of *immersionist* versions?

Dr. Cone, who was for many years President of the American and Foreign Bible Society, and also President of the American Bible Union from its organization to the time of his death, declares that the American and Foreign Bible Society was organized "to *vindicate a principle;*" that, "in accordance with *this principle*, *baptizo* and its cognates should be translated by words signifying *immerse,*" etc.

If this be true, (and no one can doubt that Dr. Cone knew for what purpose the Society was organized,) how can this Society be satisfied with any thing short of versions made upon this principle? And we have the very highest authority to prove that they are carrying out this principle in their translations into foreign tongues. What was the character of Judson's version into the Burmese tongue, and of Pearse and Yates's into the Bengalee, and also of the version into the Siamese, from which we have given quotations in this work? What is the character of the Italian and Spanish versions, specimens of which are published by the American Bible Union? Why, they are all *immersionist* versions. Dr. Cone, in a speech before the American Bible Union, in 1850, complaining of the American and Foreign Bible Society for deciding to be content with the common version in English, thus speaks: "Having directed their missionaries among the heathen to translate *baptizo* and its cognates by words signifying *immerse, immersion,* etc., they cannot long continue to be so inconsistent as to despise or reject *immersion* in their own vernacular tongue."

Dr. Cone says again: "Either fear that 'the Pedobaptists will come down upon us with tremendous power,' as a distinguished brother said, or *shame,* or some other motive of which I know nothing, deters many from bearing in ENGLISH the same testimony for Christ's despised ordinance of *immersion* which *they have made it the imperative duty* of their missionaries to bear in all the languages of the heathen."

Here it is declared by one as well posted up on this subject as any man on earth, that the American and Foreign Bible Society "have directed their missionaries in foreign countries," and "made it their imperative duty, to translate BAPTIZO and its cognates by words signifying *immerse, immersion,*" etc.

And the American Bible Union must have instructed their missionaries to the same effect. For I see in specimens of the translations into the Siamese, the Italian, and the Spanish languages immerse is translated for *baptizo*. Could "*a wicked monarch*" have done more than this? They have not merely required that the translators should be true to the original, as King James did, but they have anticipated their independent and unrestrained decision, and have "*manacled*" and "*fettered*" them, to use their own classical phraseology, so that they are constrained to put words for *baptizo* which signify *immerse*.

And from the specimens referred to above, it seems that "instead of performing the work according to the best of their knowledge and skill," they have been "obliged to submit themselves as passive instruments in the hands," not of a monarch but of associations "noted for passion, pedantry, and self-will;" and also for bigotry and exclusiveness, and the most unmitigated slander of good men and their work, in order to carry their point.

On account of the instructions those translators have received from their masters and dictators, "they do not feel at liberty" to translate *baptizo* by any word that does not signify *immerse*.

These societies do not, it seems, wish the meaning of the word *baptizo* to be known: their translators acquiesce; "and so," if they do not "*wrap it up*,". they reject it, and substitute another meaning in the place of it.

The American Bible Union was organized because the American and Foreign Bible Society would not go far enough in carrying out the great "*principle*" upon which it was organized, viz., "that baptizo and its cognates should be rendered by words signifying immerse," etc. And yet they say this is not the main object of the movement at all. All they are aiming at is to secure "*faithful versions.*"

The American Bible Union "must come to the help of the Lord against the mighty," "and show to all who understand our language that *baptism is immersion only.*" And yet they say this is not the thing they are aiming to do at all.

Dr. Cone says if it is right to preach immersion, "*it is right to print it*—TO PRINT IT IN THE BIBLE; for if it is not in the Bible, it is not right to preach it nor print it." And yet they say they do not know how the matter will turn out. They presume the translators will do justice to the meaning of the original. Their translators of the Scriptures into foreign tongues are putting words which signify *immerse* only in the place of *baptizo*, and they are publishing in their organ, the Bible Union Reporter, specimens with this peculiarity. And yet they disclaim the sectarian character of the movement.

As regards the translation of the Scriptures into English, as carried forward by the American Bible Union, it is a matter of no importance whom they have employed or may employ as translators—whether Baptists or Pedobaptists— their version must be an *immersionist* version.

They may have committed the translation of those portions containing *baptizo* and its cognates to those translators who are immersionists in principle and theory. And the Pedobaptist translators may have had committed to them no portion of the Scriptures involving the real issue. If this be the case, the translation will be a sectarian version, though Pedobaptists, as individuals on their own responsibility, may, "under written contract" for the sake of the pay, be employed.

But let this be as it may, the version must be *immersionist* in its character.

They say: "All the revisors are distinguished scholars, and men of eminent ability;" "and this is asserted and reiterated, I suppose to give confidence that the work will be done in a workmanlike manner. But all this is just no guaranty at all. For the work is to be just what the Board of Managers, Messrs. Cone, Wyckoff, and Co., would have it, or it will not be at all. They must approve it finally before it goes forth to the world; so that they will be, in fact, the only responsible authors of it, at last. Let the reader mark the following language of the Fifth Annual Report of the American Bible Union : 'Every book of the New Testament has been revised by scholars, and the manuscripts are in the possession of the Board. Of a considerable portion we have also duplicate revisions. Still, the work is by no means done. Your Board have directed their committee on versions to examine carefully each manuscript, and to recommend none for the press, unless they are satisfied that the revision possesses such a degree of merit that its publication will do honor to the Union. Otherwise it merely serves as aid to other revisors, who will do the work more thoroughly.'

"Here we have it, and in language that admits of no mistake. Every book of the New Testament has been already revised by scholars—and the manuscripts are in the possession of the Board. The *scholars* have done their part. But 'still the work is by no means done.' The Board have yet to revise the revision, and pass their judgment upon it. The committee on versions must carefully examine each manuscript, and are directed not even to print any portion, unless in their judgment it is *faithful*. *They* are to judge of '*the degree of merit*' which any and every portion of the work may possess; and none are to see the light unless they are satisfied! And who are '*they?*' Mingled emotions of indignation, contempt, and pity, must fill the bosom of the enlightened friend of Revelation on reading such pretensions from such a source. They boast of the eminent ability of the 'distinguished scholars' 'under written contract to do their work,' and make a great 'show of generosity and catholicity' in confiding the work to men holding their ecclesiastical connections with eight [*nine* now] denominations; and yet very carefully reserve to themselves the privilege of supervising each manuscript, and of judging of its merits, and throwing it aside 'if they are not *satisfied.*'"—(Dr. A. Newton, in the True Baptist.)

I would here make this inquiry, as of primary importance: Are there any Pedobaptists belonging to this committee on revision? Or are there any in the Board of Managers?

What though there should be Pedobaptists in the company of translators, this committee have the prerogative of determining what the version shall be in all its parts.

They complain of the arbitrary power exercised in giving character to the common version. But did King James assume the prerogative of revising the work of his translators? Or did he appoint a committee to do it?

Here is, under the circumstances, a most remarkable feature in "the greatest enterprise of the age," conducted by "the only people who can do justice to the subject," and "make a translation worthy of the age."

They have great confidence in their revisors, truly, that they must revise their revision, and not let it see the light unless it suits *them!*

And if they make it to suit *them,* the reader sees very clearly what kind of a one it will be. If any proposition can be proved, we think this is proved: That, whoever the translators are, or may be, whether Baptists or Pedobaptists, the purpose is settled to substitute *immerse* for *baptize.* To prove this, we have relied mainly on the friends of the new version movement.

And yet the very men whose testimony we have quoted to prove this have disclaimed it, but in some instances, in the very same connection, they have admitted it again. They *"blow hot and cold out of the same mouth"* all the time. And no wonder. The nature of their position constrains them to do so. They have two parties in their own ecclesiastical ranks to conciliate—the ultra immersionists on the one hand, and the moderate on the other. They must assert the main design clearly enough to please the former; and they must disclaim it enough to avoid, as far as possible, offending the latter.

They remind one of the fable of the farmer and the fox. Reynard, pursued by the huntsmen, and finding that he was in danger of being taken, passing by a farmer's premises, requested that he might have refuge in his barn; and that when the huntsmen should pass, and inquire if he had seen him, he should reply that he knew nothing of him. He consented, and agreed not to tell where he was. Reynard had scarcely secured his retreat, when on came the huntsmen, and inquired of the farmer if he had seen any thing of a fox passing that way. The farmer, true to his promise, *told* them that he had not, but at the same time he *pointed* very significantly toward the barn. The huntsmen catching the idea, made search, and took poor Reynard.

Thus the advocates of this movement disclaim most lustily that the design is to put *immerse* in the place of *baptize*. But, at the same time, they keep pointing most significantly in this very direction. If they are determined, like the Papists, Socinians, Universalists, Swedenborgians, Destructionists, etc., to have a version conformed to their views of biblical interpretation, let them candidly acknowledge it, and let them defend it upon its real merits. Let the public know where to find them.

CHAPTER IX.

AD HOMINEM ARGUMENT OF THE REVISIONISTS.

In this chapter I resume and continue a notice of the expedients which are adopted for the purpose of securing favor for this movement.

How natural for men to seek to justify themselves by endeavoring to show that others have done or are doing, as they have done or are doing!

This fact is very prominent in the defence which is made for the new version movement. Its friends seek to make the impression that the American Bible Society, in which all the orthodox Pedobaptist denominations are represented, have recently made a new version of the Bible; and, therefore, they argue that Pedobaptists cannot, with any consistency, complain that they are striving to secure one.

Now, if it could be established that the American Bible Society have really made a new version of the Holy Scriptures, this could not of itself justify immersionists in making one; especially, such a one as we have proved they are seeking to secure.

But to the allegation. From a tract, written by Rev. Dr. Lynd, and published by the American Bible Union, I make the following quotations:

"Let all revision men throughout Christendom reject the new edition by the American Bible Society; . . . so that it never can become 'the commonly received version.' Let us use the old editions until a pure version can be obtained."

"What authority has the American Bible Society to impose their revision upon the Churches of Christ?"

"Let their [the Baptists'] motto be, 'No revision, or a perspicuous and faithful version.'"

"Ah! it is enough to make the heart sick to hear of opposition to a revised English Bible, by the very persons who intend to use and circulate hereafter the revised editions of the American Bible Society."

I quote again from a speech of the Rev. Mr. Backus, before the American Bible Union, as published in the Bible Union Reporter for January, 1855: "We are doing just what the best of men have done before us—trying to make perfect our version of the Holy Scriptures; and whoever condemns us for so doing, must be prepared to condemn with us Wycliffe and Tyndale—those men of God to whom we are so largely indebted for our already excellent version of the Scriptures. Yes, and Coverdale, and Cranmer, and Parker, with the bishops and King James's revisors, *and the managers of the American Bible Society*, must all fall under the same *censure*, for these have all, at one time or another, been guilty of the same thing."

The design of this language is, I fear, to make a false impression. It is true, Dr. L. calls the edition of the Holy Scriptures lately published by the American Bible Society a "*revision;*" and he admits that the friends of the Bible Union are seeking a "*version.*" But this care in the use of terms is observed only in order that they may not be involved in difficulties, or may have a chance of explaining out; while the evident tendency is to make the impression that the American Bible Society have made *a new translation* of the Holy Scriptures.

The Rev. Mr. Backus is much more cautious in the use of language. He contends that the friends of this new version movement are only seeking to improve the common version: that they have precedent for this: that even the American Bible Society have set them a precedent.

Now, here is an effort to keep out of view a main point; and that is, that the *improvement* (?) mainly sought in this movement is the substitution of *immerse* and its cognates, in the Bible, for *baptize;* and thus make the Bible sectarian in its teachings. But have the American Bible Society done this? Have they made a sectarian version? Have they made any version at all?

The following quotation from the Report of the American Bible Society for 1852, page 33, will show what was contemplated in the incipiency of the measure:

"In one of the late reports, the managers

stated that, with all the pains taken to keep the text of the English Bible correct, it was found that minor differences existed in different copies issued by the Society, and also among those published by the several presses in England. Although these different readings did not affect the sense, as they pertained mostly to *orthography, italic words, capital letters,* and *punctuation,* yet it seemed highly important that there should be, if possible, uniformity in these particulars. They were specially desirous that the copies issued by the Society should be correct, and in harmony with one another. The committee on versions, composed of several different denominations— some of the members familiar with investigations of this kind—were instructed to take measures for a careful collation of the Society's Bibles, and those issued by the British and Foreign Bible Society."

I have before me the Report of the Committee on Versions, adopted May 1, 1851, after the work of collation had been completed.

From this report we learn that, in accordance

with the above instructions, the Committee on Versions, after various meetings, fixed upon the following rules, which should serve for guidance in the work of collation; and it will be observed that in these rules the instructions of the Board to the Committee are fully recognized, and are not transcended:

"1. The royal octavo edition of the English Bible, issued by the Society, be adopted as the basis for corrections.

"2. That the said American copy be compared with recent copies of the four leading British editions, viz., those of London, Oxford, Cambridge, and Edinburgh, and also with the original edition of 1611.

"3. That the comparison include the *orthography, the capital letters, words in italic, punctuation, contents of the chapters*, and running *heads* of the columns.

"4. That so far as the four English copies are *uniform*, the American copy be conformed to them, unless otherwise specially ordered by the Committee.

180 IMMERSIONISTS AGAINST THE BIBLE.

"5. That the collator be instructed, in his further labors, [this rule was adopted after the work was begun,] to apply the principles and cases previously adopted and decided by this Committee, and that, therefore, he lay before the Committee only such cases as have not before been acted upon, or such as may seem to need further consideration.

"6. That in respect to the indefinite article, the form *an* to be used before all vowels and diphthongs not pronounced as consonants, and also before *h* silent or unaccented; and that the form *a* be employed in all other cases.

"7. That in cases where the four recent British copies, and also the original edition and our own copy, vary in *punctuation*, the uniform usage of any three of the copies shall be followed.

"8. That, when the London, the Oxford, and Cambridge editions agree in the use or omission of the hyphen in compound words, the same usage to be adopted.

"9. That when the term *scripture* or *scriptures* refers to the whole volume of inspired truth, it begin with a capital letter; but when the reference is to some particular portion, it begin with a small letter."

It is proper to state that the Rev. J. W. McLane was employed as collator; and, for the greater convenience, the Committee appointed a sub-committee, consisting of Drs. Robinson and Vermilye, "to inspect the alterations suggested by the collator, and see that they are made according to the rules prescribed; and if cases of peculiar importance arise, to consult the entire Committee."

These rules show what the Committee were engaged to do—not to make or secure a new translation or version, but to make a *collation* for the purpose of correcting errors that had crept into the commonly received version.

This will appear more distinctly in the language of the Committee:

"It will be apparent, from an inspection of the rules above given, that the great and leading object of the Committee has everywhere been *uniformity*. It is only when the British copies differ that any question has been raised, except in a few instances, to be noted in the sequel. It has been the wish and endeavor of the Committee to see the English version restored, so far as possible, to its original purity, saving the necessary changes of *orthography*, and other like variations, which would assuredly be acceptable to the translators themselves, were they living at the present day. The Committee have had no authority and no desire to go behind the translators, nor in any respect to touch the original version of the text, unless in evident cases of inadvertence or inconsistency, open and manifest to all."

I will now cite a few specimens of variations secured by the Committee, to show that the design of the measure, as thus expressed, was fully maintained. I will notice each class of variations, as laid down in the report, and will select one or more specimens from each.

"1. WORDS.—In Ruth iii. 15, all the present copies read: 'And *she* went into the city;' but the Hebrew and translators have it: 'And *he* went into the city.' Again, in Cant. ii. 7, all the present copies read: 'Nor awake my love till *he* please;' but the Hebrew and the translators, 'till *she* please.' In Isaiah i. 16, the present copies read, 'Wash *you*,' where the translators put, 'Wash *ye*.' This is according to the Hebrew, and has been restored. Another change occurs in Josh. xix. 2, where the recent copies read: '*and* Sheba;' but the translators have, '*or* Sheba.' Here the Hebrew may, itself, be taken either way; but the number of thirteen cities specified in verse 6 requires *or*.

"2. ORTHOGRAPHY.—The Committee entertain a reverence for the antique forms of words and orthography in the Bible, where they do not conflict with the clear understanding of the sense. Indeed, it is such forms, in a measure, which impart an air of dignity and venerableness to our version. For this reason, phrases like, 'hoised up the mainsail,' (Acts xxvii. 40,) also words like 'graff' and 'graffed,' (Rom. xi. 17, 19, 23, 24,) have not been altered. But when these forms have become obsolete and unintelligible; or have already been changed in some places, and not in others; or when in themselves they are of no importance, there seems to be no valid reason for longer retaining them. By far the greater portion of the readers of the English Bible are unlearned persons and children; and it is essential to remove every thing in the mere form, which may become to any a stumbling-block in the way of the right and prompt understanding of God's holy word.

"The following examples still occur in the English editions; but have mostly already been changed in the Edinburgh and American copies. Many of them are variations from the edition of 1611:

	ENGLISH COPIES.	CORRECTED.
Gen. viii. 1,	asswaged.	assuaged.
" xi. 3,	morter.	mortar.
" " "	throughly.	thoroughly. (tr. Cam.)
" xxx. 35,	ringstraked.	ringstreaked.
" " 37,	strakes.	streaks.
" xxxi. 10,	grisled.	grizzled.
Ex. vi. 21,	Zithri. (prob. error of press.)	Zichri (tr. Edin.)
" xxxii. 20,	strowed.	strewed.
Lev. xiv. 42,	plaister.	plaster.

	ENGLISH COPIES.	CORRECTED.
Num. x. 25,	rereward.	rearward.
" xx. 14,	travel.	travail.
Deut. xiv. 15,	cuckow.	cuckoo.
" xv. 17,	aul.	awl.
Judges v. 22,	pransings.	prancings.
Ruth i. 18,	stedfastly.	steadfastly.
2 Sam. xv. 12,	counseller. (tr. Lond. Cam.)	counsellor.
1 Kings vi. 15,	cieling. (tr. sicling)	ceiling.
2 Chron. ii. 16,	flotes.	floats.
Neh. ix. 1,	sackclothes.	sackcloth. (as in Joel i. 13.)
Isa. xli. 2,	sodering.	soldering.
Jer. ii. 22,	sope.	soap.
Ezra xl. 31,	utter court.	outer court.
Zech. xi. 13,	prised.	prized.
Matt. xxvii. 48,	spunge.	sponge.
Acts vii. 28,	diddest.	didst.
Eph. v. 8,	sometimes.	sometime. (i. e., once, formerly.)
1 Tim. ii. 9,	broidered. (tr. broided.)	braided.
Rev. xiv. 20,	horse bridles.	horses' bridles. (so the Greek.)

"A variation likewise occurs in the mode of writing the *imperfect* and *participle* of many verbs; all of which have been corrected to the present standard. The following are examples:

Gen. viii. 11, 'pluckt;' but 'plucked,' Deut. xxviii. 63. Gen. xviii. 7, 'fetcht;' but in verse 4, 'fetched.' Gen. xxi. 7, 'have born,' in recent copies; the translators, correctly, 'have borne.' Deut. ii. 37, 'forbad,' in recent copies; the translators, correctly, 'forbade.' Ezra ix. 3, 'astonied;' and so in all the copies: Job xviii. 20; Ezra iv. 17; Dan. iii. 24, etc. In some passages this has been already changed to 'astonished,' as in Job xvii. 8.

"In expressing the plurals of such Hebrew words as are not rendered in the text, the translators adopted the plural form of the Hebrew in *im*, but with the superfluous addition of *s*; as *cherubims*, *seraphims*, *Nethimims*, *Anakims*, etc. This is strictly wrong, and is not in accordance with present usage. The *s* has therefore everywhere been dropped in such words: as Gen. iii. 24, Isa. vi. 2, 6, etc.

"In respect to the *particles of exclamation*, *O* and *Oh*, it appears, on examination, that the former (*O*) is everywhere used before a vocative case; while before an optative we find both: 'O that,' Deut. xxxii. 29, Ps. lv. 6; and 'Oh that,' Job vi. 2, Jer. ix. 1. In order to maintain the proper distinction, the form *Oh* has everywhere been retained with the optative, leaving *O* as the sign of the vocative.

"The forms of the indefinite article *a* or *an* have been adjusted throughout according to the sixth rule above given. In order to show the necessity of the rule, the following examples of inconsistency in all the copies, from first to last, are here selected:

"Gen. xxv. 25, 'an hairy;' Gen. xxvii. 11, 'a hairy.' Judges iv. 21, 'an hammer;' Jer. xxiii. 29, 'a hammer.' Isa. xi. 16, 'an highway;' Is. xix. 23, 'a highway.' Matt. x. 12, 'an house;' Mark iii. 25, 'a house.' Ruth i. 12, 'an husband;' Ruth i. 12, 'a husband.'

"2. PROPER NAMES.—There exists in the Old Testament a very considerable diversity in the mode of writing Hebrew proper names in English. Thus, the names of the first seven patriarchs of the world, as they appear in Gen., chap. iv., and as they are now usually written, are:

Adam, Seth, Enos, Cainan, Mahalaleel, Jared, Enoch. But in 1 Chron. i. 1, sq., the same are recorded as: Adam, Sheth, Enosh, Kenan, Mahalaleel, Jered, Henoch; the Hebrew forms being in both places precisely the same. This is but a single specimen, and shows at least an inadvertence on the part of the translators. In some instances, also, there is a slight difference even in the Hebrew forms themselves, in different books. In cases like the preceding, involving, as they do, a difference of pronunciation, the Committee have not felt themselves authorized to make any change, regarding the great principle of uniformity in the copies as of higher importance.

"In the New Testament the case is somewhat different. Here it is to be regretted, that in respect to persons *already known in the Old Testament*, the translators did not retain their names in the form in which they had thus become familiar. Instead of this, they have introduced the personages of ancient Jewish history under names modified, and sometimes disguised, by transmission through the Greek tongue. Thus, in Acts vii 45, and Heb. iv. 8, we find the name *Jesus*, which the common reader will naturally refer only to the Saviour; while in reality it is simply the Greek form for *Joshua*, and should properly have been so written. In the same way the name *Core* in Jude 11 is unintelligible to most readers; for comparatively few would ever suspect its identity with Korah of the Old Testament. So, too, the translators have sometimes taken the form of the Greek genitive *Juda*, *Jona*, to represent the Hebrew names *Judah*, *Jonah*.

"The principle adopted in such cases has been the following: When such names occur singly in the narrative, and there would arise no marked difference in the pronunciation, the form in the Old Testament has been restored. The name *Jesus*, as above cited, is explained in the margin by the translators themselves. The following are examples:

FORMER READING.	CORRECTED.
Matt. ii. 6, Juda.	Judah.
" x. 15, Gomorrha.	Gomorrah

FORMER READING.	CORRECTED.
Matt. xxi. 5, Sion.	Zion.
" xxiv. 37, Noe.	Noah.
Acts vii. 11, Chanaan.	Canaan.
" vii. 30, Sina.	Sinai.
Heb. xi. 11, Sara.	Sarah.
Rev. ii. 14, Balac.	Balak.

"3. COMPOUND WORDS.—The eighth rule prescribes that the usage of the English copies be followed in respect to the insertion or omission of the hyphen in compound words. It was found that the Edinburgh and American copies employ the hyphen in very many instances where, by the operation of the rule, it has been dropped. In such cases, generally, the words have afterwards been written as *one* word, or as *two* words, according as the accent in pronunciation is placed upon the first word, or otherwise. Thus, *bedchamber, handmaid;* but *meat offering, burnt sacrifice* This accords for the most part with the English copies.

"4. CAPITAL LETTERS.—The ninth rule provides for the manner of writing the term *scrip-*

ture and *scriptures*, with or without a capital letter. A similar rule has been followed in practice in respect to the word "*Spirit*," which everywhere is made to begin with a capital when it refers to the Spirit of God as a Divine Agent; but not when it denotes other spiritual beings, or the spirit of man. The following is a specimen of the changes which have been made:

ENGLISH COPIES.	CORRECTED.
Gen. vi. 3, My spirit.	My Spirit.
(So too Gen. xli. 38:	Num. xxiv. 2.)
Ps. xxi. 7, most High.	Most High.
Isa. lxiii. 10, holy Spirit.	Holy Spirit.
Rev. iv. 5, seven Spirits of God.	seven spirits of God.

"5. WORDS IN ITALICS.—These were inserted by the translators to fill out the English idiom, in cases where the Hebrew and Greek usage omits the copula or other connecting or dependent words. These insertions were carefully revised and compared with the original by Dr. Blaney; but notwithstanding his diligence, quite a number of errors have been detected, some of which belong to the translators. The following are examples:

"Ex. viii. 21, 22, 24, 29, 31. Here the recent copies all read, 'swarms *of flies;*' while in Ps. lxxviii. 45, and cv. 31, the same Hebrew word is rendered, 'divers sorts of flies,' without italics. In all these passages the edition of 1611 has no italics.

"Judges ix. 53. The edition of 1611 and all others read: 'And all to break his skull.' This has been often misunderstood, and has been sometimes printed: 'And all to brake.' But 'all to' is an antique form, signifying 'altogether,' and was last so used by Milton. It here gives an emphasis to 'brake' which is not in Hebrew. The Committee have therefore put *all-to* in italics, with a hyphen, and have inserted a note of explanation in the margin.

"Luke i. 35: 'Which shall be born of thee.' So in all the copies first and last; but the words *of thee* should be in italic; there being nothing corresponding in the Greek.

"John x. 28, 29: 'Any man . . . . no man.'

So in the edition of 1611. The Oxford copy rightly reads, 'Any *man* . . . . no *man;*' the Edinburgh and American have, 'any . . . none,' corrected, like the Oxford, 'any *man* . . . . no *man.*'

"6. PUNCTUATION.—It was found that the three English copies have a general uniformity in respect to punctuation, especially in the frequent use of the colon; while the Edinburgh and American often prefer the semicolon, and are in general more conformed to the edition of 1611. The seventh rule prescribes that 'the uniform usage of any *three* of the copies shall be followed.' · In the great majority of instances, the operation of the rule has produced conformity with the English copies. In cases where the rule was not applicable, the Committee have endeavored to decide each according to its merits.

"The following five changes made in the punctuation, are all, it is believed, which affect the sense :

"Rom. iv. 1 : 'That Abraham, our father as pertaining to the flesh, hath found.' Here, according to the order of the Greek, it should read: 'hath found as pertaining to the flesh.' The true pointing, therefore, is a comma after Abraham, and another after father. This is found in no edition hitherto.

"1 Cor. xvi. 22: 'Let him be Anathema Maran-atha.' There should be a period after Anathema, which no edition inserts. The two words 'maran atha' are simply an Aramean formula, signifying 'The Lord cometh.' Compare Phil. iv. 5.

"2 Cor. x. 8–11. All the copies now have a colon after verse 8, and a period after verse 9, connecting the two verses in sense. The true pointing, however, is a period after verse 8, and then a colon after verse 9, and also verse 10; thus connecting verse 9 as protasis with verse 11 as apodasis. So Chrysostom, and so the Syriac and Latin versions; and this is required by the logical sequence.

"Heb. xiii. 7. Here should be a period at the end of the verse after conversation.' So the translators, the Oxford and other copies. The Edinburgh and American have sometimes a colon, and sometimes a comma.

"Rev. xiii. 8. Here a comma is inserted after 'slain;' since the qualification 'from the foundation of the world' refers not to 'slain,' but to 'written;' as is shown by the parallel verse, Rev. xvii. 8 : the translators wrongly insert a comma after 'Lamb;' others put no stop at all.

"7. PARENTHESES.—Our collation has shown that very many parentheses have been introduced into the text since the edition of 1611. Some of these are fit and proper; but in general they only mar the beauty of the page, without adding any thing to perspicuity. In some instances, too, they have the force of commentary. For these reasons, those not inserted by the translators have been in great part omitted : as in Rom. v. 13–17; xi. 8 : 2 Cor. xii. 2 : Gal. i. 1 : Rev. ii. 9, etc.

"8. BRACKETS.—These are found but once—1 John ii. 23, enclosing the last clause of the verse, which the translators put in *italics*. This was done because that clause was not then contained in the received text of the Greek New Testament;

although the sense requires it, and it was read in the best manuscripts and in the versions. The clause is now inserted in all critical editions of the Greek Testament; and, as there is no question of its genuineness, both the brackets and the *italics* have been dropped."

These examples are sufficient to show the nature of the work which the American Bible Society have secured. I might have given specimens of the changes made in the contents of the chapters, the running heads of the columns, the marginal readings and references, and chronology; but as these do not affect the text, it is not necessary to do so.

The Committee use the following language in closing their report: "Such is the account which the Committee have to render to the Board of Managers, of their stewardship in this work; although this account, and the few specimens above presented, can of course afford no adequate idea of the time, the attention, and the labor bestowed on the work by the sub-committee and the collator during the period of three years. And now, invoking the continued blessing of the Most High, and with a deep sense of their own imperfections, the Committee would commend the result of their labors to the favorable consideration of the Board, as also of the Society, and of the Christian public. They claim no special freedom from error: they may, very possibly, not always have fully carried out their own rules: they may have committed oversights. But they shrink from no responsibility; and they have no desire to cover up, either what they have done, or what they have left undone. The thing has not been done in a corner.

"As illustrating the necessity of the present collation, and the remarks already made upon the exposure to variation and error in the printing of so many millions of copies, it may suffice here to mention that the number of variations recorded by the collator, solely in the text and punctuation of the six copies compared, falls but little short of *twenty-four thousand*. Yet of all this great number, there is not one which mars the integrity of the text, or affects any doctrine or precept of the Bible.

"In thus closing their labors, the Committee desire, with grateful praise to God, distinctly and formally to state, that *no decision whatever has been made, and nothing whatever has been done, except with* ENTIRE UNANIMITY *on the part of the Committee and those acting with them.*"

It is proper to give the reader the names of the eminent men composing the Committee on Versions, and which are appended to the report from which we have made the above quotations. They are as follows: Gardiner Spring, Thomas Cock, Samuel H. Turner, Edward Robinson, Thomas E. Vermilye, John McClintock, Richard S. Storrs.

I will conclude on this point with a few remarks:

1. The work accomplished under the auspices of the American Bible Society is not a *version* or *translation* at all, but a *collation*. Let this be noted by the reader. Collation, as used in this case, means comparison of some six editions of the English Bible, embracing the edition of 1611 as the standard, for the purpose of correcting

errors which had accidentally crept into the Scriptures. There was no *translation* from the original Hebrew and Greek, but a mere correction of errors that had gotten into a translation already made and acknowledged as the standard. The object of the Committee simply, to use their own language, " was to restore the English version to its original purity." They affirm that they " had no authority and no desire to go behind the translators, nor in any respect to touch the original version of the text."

Except in *orthography* and inadvertencies open and manifest to all, they have not touched the original version. · This is fully and strikingly illustrated in the foregoing specimens of the variations they have made. In this respect, what the American Bible Society have done is entirely different from what the American Bible Union are engaged in doing. They have denounced the common version as unfaithful to the original; and are seeking a new version, which, as they claim, will be a more faithful exhibition of the original Scriptures.

2. The work accomplished by the American Bible Society is not *sectarian* in its character. The learned men employed in the collation belong to and represented the denominations who patronize the Society. And we learn from their reports that every thing they did was agreed upon "with ENTIRE UNANIMITY," and then finally approved and adopted by the Board of Managers and the whole Society. But is the translation sought by the American Bible Union to be non-sectarian in its character? If any proposition can be proved, we have already proved, by an amount and character of evidence perfectly overwhelming to the unprejudiced mind, that this new version movement was conceived in a desire to put *immerse* and its cognates in the place of *baptize* and its cognates; and that it has been prosecuted up to this time mainly for the accomplishment of this object.

Let the enemies of the common version show one instance in which a change has been made in the common version that favors any sectarian view or usage. They cannot do this. And yet they are endeavoring to make use of the fact of the collation of the Scriptures by the American Bible Society as excuse for them in what they are doing. They are very much concerned to get a cloak to cover their misdoing. They cannot get the American Bible Society to help bear the fearful responsibility they have incurred. They will be constrained to meet it unaided. The old adage that "a drowning man will catch at a straw," is very forcibly illustrated in the manner in which this movement is advocated. Its friends seem to doubt its intrinsic merits, and, therefore, the fallacious use of the *argumentum ad hominem*. A specimen of this sophism has already been noticed in this chapter. Before we close it, we will notice another specimen.

It is stated that all the principal Pedobaptist denominations have had their denominational versions of the Holy Scriptures: that Doddridge, Macknight, and George Campbell, have made translations for the Presbyterians: that Wesley has made a translation for the Methodists, etc.

Now, we admit that Doddridge, Macknight.

Wesley, and other learned men, have made translations of the Holy Scriptures. But did they design that they should be recognized as the standards of the denominations to which they belonged? Did they ever intimate any such thing at any time? Did the denominations to which these men belonged think of receiving their versions in the place of the common version?

These men made their translations as individuals. In making them, they were not considered by themselves, nor their denominations, nor the world, as doing their work, however praiseworthy it might be in itself, at the bidding or request of the Churches to which they belonged. Where is there in Mr. Wesley's translation, for instance, any thing indicating that he expected or desired that it should displace the common version? At what time and at what place did the Methodists, in any form or manner, intimate that they desired to displace the translation of King James with Mr. Wesley's?

It is true that both the preachers and people

have read Mr. Wesley's translation of the New Testament, as they have read his Notes, Sermons, etc., simply as the production of a learned and good man. But they have never recognized him, nor do they recognize him as a standard translator. The same remarks are applicable to the translations of other learned Pedobaptist authors. But admitting, for the sake of argument, that these versions are the standards of the denominations with which their authors were identified, they were not designed merely to subserve the interests of their denominational theories and practice. As far as the versions of Doddridge and Macknight are concerned, they are, in some respects, decidedly unfavorable to Presbyterian practice.

In Wesley's version, in what single instance is there a variation from the common version favoring the peculiar theory and usages of the author and his sect?

But we have proved that a distinctive feature in the version the immersionists are seeking, is the substitution of *immerse* for *baptize*, so that their peculiar usage may have the authority of *Scripture,* though it may be *Baptist Scripture* after all.

If these revisionists had adduced the case of the Papists, Swedenborgians, Unitarians, Universalists, Destructionists, etc., as having secured versions to sustain their peculiar theories, the cases would have been much more apposite. The Bible of the Papists has *penance* instead of *repentance;* and so of the others. The Baptist Bible will have no *baptism* in it, but *immerse* instead of it.

Our new version friends have "*precedent*" truly for revision. In this age of improvement, when a fanatical sect cannot prove their ultraisms from the common version, they at once put it on the rack, and constrain it to testify in their favor. The Baptists and Campbellites are endeavoring to keep up with the times. They will not be fully up, however, till they get a new Bible entire from heaven, or some other source, like the Mormons.

Conybeare and Howson, in their late learned

and able work, "The Life and Epistles of St. Paul," have been quoted as translators in favor of revision.

But to show the utter recklessness of the advocates of this movement, I quote from vol. i., p. 18, Introd. They give in the introduction the reasons of their making a translation of Paul's epistles. It was not on account of any low opinion of the common version. For they say, as if they had in mind the temerity of our revisionists in publishing their version, as they are doing, alongside the common version: It is "a rash experiment to provoke such a contrast between the *matchless style* of the authorized version and that of the modern translator, thus placed side by side."

They justify their translation solely on the ground that they had a special object in view, which could only be accomplished by a paraphrase; and it is evident that they rest much of the value of their work upon their paraphrastic skill, which is, they admit, rather the merit of the commentator than of the translator. They evidently intend to convey the idea that the authorized version is to be held in estimation for its great faithfulness to the original as it is, and not as sectarians would suppose it should be.

Hence they say, "If the text admit of two interpretations, our version (the common) endeavors, if possible, to preserve the same ambiguity, and effects this often with admirable skill." This they characterize as "a merit in an authorized version."

The design of the authorized version is, they say, to make "a standard of authority, and ultimate appeal in controversy." This they give as the reason of its great faithfulness to the original. This fidelity, they admit, is the occasion of difficulties; but they add, "Had any other course been adopted, every sect would have had its own Bible: as it is, this one translation has been all but unanimously received for three centuries:" (two and a half they should have said.)

The general conclusion of these learned men, in their apology for a new version of Paul's epistles, is, that the authorized version is inimitable and unapproachable as a standard, and that new versions or translations should only have in view a special purpose, which, of course, is to be judged of by circumstances: should always be avowed unambiguously; and should be permitted to pass the ordeal of public opinion. They avow the purpose of their work to be " to give a living picture of the Apostle Paul himself, and the circumstances by which he was surrounded." The work is a biography of the apostle. Much that is peculiar to him is contained in his epistles. A new version is resorted to for the purpose of catching what the versionist supposes to be the spirit of the apostle.

CHAPTER X.

CHANGES PROPOSED IN THE COMMON VERSION.

I HAVE already demonstrated that the main design of this movement is to substitute *immerse* for *baptize;* yet as a great many changes have been proposed, though merely to gain favor for the substitution of *immerse*, it may be proper to notice some of them. Let it be borne in mind that we have never denied that the common version has defects. This has all along been admitted. And this is true of all the versions that have ever been made; and it will be true of any that may yet be made. In the language of the Rev. Mr. Hodge, a Baptist minister of Brooklyn, N. Y., "A man who could remove every fault, and produce a perfect translation, would be able to kindle a comet and send it blazing through the heavens." And were the position assumed and acted upon, that no translation that is not perfect, and especially that all evangelical Christians would regard as perfect, should be patronized, we should be constrained to let the revelation of God remain in the original tongues, or cease the work of Bible distribution altogether. Says Dr. Williams, who, though a Baptist, is opposed to this movement: "No man will claim for the English Scriptures perfection. A perfect version is a nonentity, and we believe an impossibility, whilst imperfect and uninspired translators are the only agents to furnish it, and a living language, ever changing from the very fact of its life, remains the only material on which such translators are to work. No sober man can expect to attain, no modest nor thorough scholar would venture to promise, a version that approached immaculate perfection."

That the translation sought by the advocates of this movement will not be "*immaculate*," will appear as very likely from a slight examination of some of the changes from the common version which have been proposed. It will appear very evident that these pious Bible-menders are sadly under the deluding influence of a spirit of extravagant hypercriticism.

Much stress is laid on what they call *obsolete terms*. "*Let*," as used in Rom. i. 13, and 2 Thess. ii. 7, etc., it is said "contradicts the sense." But no intelligent reader will be in danger of misunderstanding the term. No one, not even a Sabbath-school scholar of ten years of age, will be in any danger of construing it as meaning "permit" or "allow." The very connection determines the sense. Who misunderstands the familiar phrase, "without *let* or hindrance?" "And the time will never arrive when the reader of God's word will not have occasion to exercise his discrimination; or when its language will not need to be illustrated and explained." The phrase "bid him. God speed," 2 John 10, is pronounced "*profane*" by these *holy critics*. But who but they can see any profanity in the use of the phrase, as a benediction on one supposed to be in a right course of action?

The phrase "God forbid," as a form of emphatic denial, is pronounced "an irreverent oath." And they suggest the translation of Gal. vi. 14, as follows: *"May it not be* that I should glory," etc. Dr. Williams, of New York, who, perhaps, has no superior in this country in his knowledge of English literature, shows most conclusively that there is no ground for this harsh criticism. He shows that the phrase itself is preserved in the original Hebrew, in the case of the good Naboth refusing to sell the inheritance of his fathers to Ahab, (1 Kings, xxi. 3,) and on three other occasions, as used by David, when that magnanimous saint forbore to take the life of Saul, and once when he poured out, as a drink offering, the water that had been procured at the well of Bethlehem at the risk of his warriors' lives. (1 Sam. xxiv. 6, xxvi. 11; and 1 Chron. xi. 19.)

It is argued that the original Greek phrase, μὴ γένοιτο, *me genoito,* "has not in it the idea of God;" and that "by no means," or "be it not," would be preferable to the introduction of the name of God "without any authority from Scripture." But in the sacred text itself, according to Dr. Williams, the word for the Divine Being occurs in the four passages in the Hebrew to which we have referred. And so, consequently, we have "scriptural authority" for this form of expression as translated in the common version.

The phrases suggested are utterly too tame to express "the strong and indignant disclaimer and the impetuous dislike the original phrase conveys." Our word "*never*" would better express "its passionate and impulsive negative." But this implies rather a reliance on our own strength to avert an impending evil; while the Greek phrase is rather an appeal to a higher and overruling might to avert the danger or the sin. Tholuck, on the Romans, calls it "the strongest form of negation," and gives the Hebrew term "*chalilah*" as its equivalent. The phrases proposed to be substituted for "*God forbid*" all necessarily refer the mind to a superior power, as well as this phrase. If they are not thus construed, they have no sense nor force in them; and they are consequently subject to the same objection. And if they do not refer to the true God, as the Supreme in authority and power, to whom do they refer? Do the advocates of the new version intend to establish the recognition of any other god as supreme? I think this will be equally as "*irreverent*" as the assumed use of God's name "without any scriptural authority."

The phrase "Holy Ghost," as an appellation of the third person of the Holy Trinity, is objected to, as expressing only the idea of an apparition, and as being "*manifest blasphemy.*"

Dr. Williams shows, in reply to this charge, "that the parent Anglo-Saxon had the term not only in the sense of *phantom*, but also in the general, reverent idea of '*spirit.*' The German, with which our people and literature are daily growing of closer kin and fuller acquaintance, has essentially the same word, in the large and innocuous sense. And the classics of the language—not to be extruded by our sweeping criticisms from the libraries and schools of the English race—Dryden, whose prose Fox took as the very standard of pure English, and Shakspeare, and the great Hooker, and the English

Common Prayer, all have the word 'ghostly' in the signification of spiritual and religious. To divide the appellation from the term 'Holy,' indissolubly employed with it, in our hymns and prayers and best religious writers, is neither fair criticism, nor duly reverent to the theme and Being. And would the brethren who adopt this line of argument, receive it, if their fellow-disciples, who see and feel no such unhappy associations with this term that is sacred to their hearts from their earliest and holiest recollections of it, should ask the brethren to carry out the same principle in its bearings on the other Name which the translators use for the Paraclete? Every one at all conversant with the familiar and lighter literature of our tongue, knows that, from the first Quakers down to our own time, superficial and reckless writers have delighted to confound the dread name of the third person in the Godhead with the liquid and disguised death that brims the wine-cup and enriches the dram-seller. The lighter literature of England absolutely reeks with irreverent allusions of this kind, recalling the blasphemy which the enemies of the apostles employed on the day of Pentecost, when they attributed the influences of the descended 'Spirit' to '*new wine.*' Would not the brethren .... be generally and justly wounded, if, because of those irreverent expressions, we should strive to denounce the expression itself, and employ of it strong expressions parallel to those used .... against the other Name—expressions only serving to nail on the writhing memory of the pious, profane associations with holy things—associations they would deplore and detest, and strive earnestly and prayerfully to forget for ever? We know well the brethren ... would shrink from laying a hand like Uzzah's, rash even in its honest endeavors to stay the ark, upon the cause they love."

Webster defines the phrase "Holy Ghost"— "The third person in the adorable Trinity."

But is not the phrase "Holy Spirit" obnoxious to the very same objection which they urge against "Holy Ghost?" Is not the term "*spirit,*" with which they propose translating πνεῦμα, *pneuma*, used to signify an apparition—a ghost? So says Webster; and upon their own principle, the use of the term "*spirit,*" as an appellative of the third person in the Trinity, "is manifest blasphemy." It is a matter of some interest to know what term they will secure.

The substitution of "Teacher" for "Master" is urged as "demanded" by fidelity to the truth, in John xiii. 13, 14: Matt. xvii. 24, ix. 11, x. 24: Luke vi. 40, etc.

But the slightest examination of the subject will convince any one that the full force of the original Διδάσκαλος, *Didaskalos*, is not contained in the word "teacher;" for the word implies not only one who communicates knowledge, but, in its application to Christ, it implies also *authority* as a teacher.

Webster, in defining "teacher," does not give one acceptation as involving the idea of authority or government; but in defining "master," he not only gives it as containing the idea of governing, but also as involving the idea of instructing. This, then, is the term which ought to be used, in order to express the full intent of the original word. And just let the reader test the proposed change, by substituting the word "Teacher" for "Master," in the passages above referred to, and he will see that the import is perfectly tame and insufficient.

"Make to stumble," for "offend," is proposed as a translation of σκανδαλίζω, *skandalizo*. If the rendering of the common version be obscure, as alleged, how much less obscure is this? Let the reader test it by reading a few passages with this change, viz.: " Doth this *make you stumble?*" instead of, " Doth this *offend* you?" "All ye *shall be made to stumble* this night," instead of, "All ye shall be offended," etc. " If thy right hand *make thee stumble*," etc., instead of, " If thy right hand *offend thee*," etc.

It will be observed that this proposed change is perfectly reckless of the fact that the original word in these instances, as in the common version, is not used in a *literal*, but in a *figurative* sense; and, therefore, by giving a literal sense in the translation, they pervert the meaning of the

Saviour and the apostles, and make them speak nonsense.

In Acts xvii. 22, "very religious" is proposed to be substituted for "too superstitious;" and the passage would then read: "I perceive that in all things ye are very religious."

The term in the original is a very different one from that used in James i. 26. In James, it is θρῆσκος, *threskos*. In this passage it is δεισιδαίμων, *deisidaimon*. In James, the term *threskos* means religious, devout, pious. In this passage, the term *deisidaimon* is a compound of δείδω, *deido*, to fear, and δαίμων, *daimon*, which in the New Testament usually signifies the Devil or an evil spirit; and in 1 Cor. x. 20, 21, it designates the heathen divinities—invisible objects of idolatrous worship.

We are constrained to conclude, therefore, that the translation proposed is unjustifiable. If the apostle had intended to express the idea of the Athenians being very religious in a good sense, it is strange he should not have used the same word which James uses, or one of the same import.

But who can think that the inspired apostle of the Gentiles should have adopted the expedient of bestowing a compliment on the idolatrous Athenians, for the purpose of avoiding the excitement of their prejudices against his mission? The translation of the common version is then a good one, and the one proposed is a false one, if we are to be guided by the scriptural usage of the original term.

It is proposed to substitute "sound of the voice" for "voice," in Acts ix. 7. The passage would then read: "The men who journeyed with him stood speechless, hearing *the sound of* the voice."

In reference to this change, I quote from a pamphlet containing a very able review of the New Version movement, by a committee appointed by a meeting of Baptists of the city of New York, opposed to the movement. This able document is signed by Drs. Welch, Dowling, and three others.

They use the following language, (pp. 30, 31 :) "The ground on which this alteration is defended is the use of the genitive case, instead of the accusative, in the original text. It cannot, however, have escaped the notice of an attentive reader of the Greek Testament, that, as respects *the usage of the sacred writers*, (to extend the investigation no farther,) there is not the slightest indication of any difference in the force of the two forms of expression. They are, *throughout the New Testament,* used *interchangeably*, and in all respects in such manner as to place it beyond all doubt that they were regarded as being entirely synonymous.

"The apostle, in the statement, recorded Acts xxii. 7, and xxvi. 14, "And I heard *a voice* saying unto me, Saul, Saul, why persecutest thou me?" uses in one case the genitive, and in the other the accusative.

"Again, the Apostle John, in the phrase, 'And I heard *a great voice* saying,' occurring Rev. i. 10, xvi. 1, xix. 1, xxi. 3, employs in two instances the genitive; in the other two, the accusative. Again, in Rev. x. 4, and xiv. 13, 'And I heard *a voice* from heaven saying unto me,' the genitive is used in the former passage; the accusative in the latter. And as in all these instances the very words which were spoken are recorded as having been heard and understood, it would be folly to say that the reference in the one case is simply and specifically to the *sound of the voice,* and in the other to the *voice* itself. To these may be added the passage, Heb. iii. 15: 'To-day if ye will *hear his voice,* (genitive,) harden not your hearts;' as also John xviii. 37: 'Every one that is of the truth *heareth my voice:*' language which, so far from being adapted to express or even to suggest any idea such as our brethren seek to attach to it, most obviously refers to the 'voice,' not simply as understood, but *obeyed.* See also John v. 25, x. 16, 27: 2 Tim. i. 13: Rev. iii. 20, etc.

"These facts must suffice to satisfy every mind that the distinction which our brethren *imagine* they perceive in the phraseology under consideration has not the *slightest foundation* in the usage of the New Testament writers. And we cannot but regard the introduction of the words, 'the sound of,' into Acts ix. 7, as being, in the view of this usage, not an 'amendment,' or improvement in the translation, but an unwarranted 'addition' to the sacred text. No one, however respectable may be his attainments in classic Greek, can be justified in undertaking the work of translating the New Testament, without first becoming thoroughly acquainted with the scriptural usage; and the usage, too, which in each case may serve to illustrate the import of the particular passage to be translated. Far less are the sweeping denunciations of the received translation, as being 'palpably' erroneous, in which our brethren have so freely indulged, to be excused, when, as in the present case, a little examination is sufficient to place it beyond all dispute, that the 'erroneousness' in reality and manifestly pertains to what is offered as a 'correction' or 'amendment.'

"With regard to the import of Acts ix. 7, we see no occasion for setting aside the idea naturally suggested to the mind by the received translation; especially when it is considered that there is nothing in the passage to indicate that the men in company with Saul understood the import of what was uttered, (comp. chap. xvi. 14,) or *to whom, or by whom* it was spoken."

"In prison," is proposed for "in hold"—Acts iv. 3; and the passage would then read: "And they laid hands on them and put them *in prison* unto the next day." The original word, τήρησις, *teresis*, (from τηρέω, *tereo*, to have an eye to, to watch, to keep, to guard,) is defined by Robinson as to its use in the New Testament: 1. A watching, keeping—3. guard, watch; in New Testament, *meton., place of ward*, prison: Greenfield, *a keeping, custody, i. e., by meton.*, a place where one is confined, prison, hold, ward.

It will be observed, then, that whenever this term is used to signify prison, or place of custody, it is so used by *metonymy*. Its proper meaning is *safe keeping, custody;* and this sense is certainly very suitable for Acts iv. 3. No improvement can be realized by substituting the *figurative* for the *primary, literal* sense of the term. And the perspicuity of the passage does not require it.

"Faithless" is proposed to be substituted "for believe not," in 2 Tim. ii. 13 : "If we *believe not*, yet he abideth faithful : he cannot deny himself;" which, *when improved*, will read : "If we be *faithless*, he abideth faithful," etc.

On this, Messrs. Welch, Dowling, etc., remark: "The *idea* expressed by the passage, as it stands in our present version, is one of peculiar interest and force, to wit : our unbelief or incredulity respecting the Divine declarations cannot do away with the certainty of their fulfilment. His revealed purposes, whether regarded or disregarded, will, without the possibility of a failure, be executed: to distrust his word, although it may awaken a temporary feeling of security, will be unavailing in the end, inasmuch as he is faithful to his word : *he cannot deny himself*. The substitution of the word *faithless*, however, in the sense *false to one's trust and profession*—the sense evidently intended, as furnishing the only ground on which a change in the translation could be supposed to be necessary—entirely changes the import and bearing of the passage, and leaves us with a sense which will, we believe, be generally regarded as being, in comparison with the one which we have indicated, tame and frigid. Indeed, it is not a little difficult to perceive what relation our unfaithfulness sustains to the faithfulness of God. What, then, is the ground on which the substitution is made?

"It will doubtless excite the surprise of those not acquainted with the original text, to learn that the sense presented in this so-called 'amendment,' which is at variance with what *seems* to be required by the scope and design of the passage, so far from being 'demanded,' or even suggested by the established import of the original term, is secured only by the actual rejection of its *uniform* meaning, as occurring in other passages in the New Testament. The compound word *apisteo* is always used by the sacred writers in the sense 'believe not;' as, for example, in Acts xxviii 24: 'And some believed the things which were spoken, and some *believed not.*' Mark xvi. 16: 'He that *believeth not* shall be damned.' Luke xxiv. 41: 'While they *believed not* for joy.' Rom. iii. 3: 'What if some did *not believe,*' etc. The noun *apistia* is likewise generally used in the same characteristic import; as in Rom. iv. 20: 'He staggered not at the promise of God through *unbelief.*' See also Mark vi. 6: Matt. xiii. 58, xvii. 20: Rom. xi. 20, etc. And even the adjective form, *apistos*, is usually employed in the New Testament, not in the sense *faithless* or unfaithful, as contrasted with faithful, but as meaning *unbelieving, without faith.* See 1 Cor. vii. 14: '*The unbelieving* husband;' x. 27; xiv. 22, 23, etc. And yet, in opposition to the evidence afforded by these facts, as well as in opposition to what *we* regard as the exigencies of the passage itself, the sense 'believe not' is expunged from 2 Tim. ii. 13, and one which is favored by no parallel passage in the New Testament is introduced in its stead; and all this, we are left to infer, as the correction of a 'gross' and 'palpable' error."

Errors in grammar, of fearful enormity, have been charged upon the common version. The first class of these sins against Priscian includes the use of "*be*" for "*are.*" Says Dr. Williams: "Now, to put this ancient form of expression, common to some of the best of the elder classics of the language, under the caption of 'grammatical errors,' argues great heedlessness or temerity." He then quotes Lord Bacon as using it, as follows: "Certainly there *be* that delight in giddiness."

A second class of sins against the laws of grammar, includes the use of "which" for "who." But Lord Bacon is again cited. He uses the following, as quoted by Dr. Williams: "The apostles and disciples *which* saw our Saviour in the flesh."

The use of the preposition "for," before the infinitive, is charged as "erroneous and clumsy;" but Webster says that "the use is *correct*, though now obsolete."

These are but specimens of the changes proposed; but they are sufficient to show that the advocates of this movement are pressed for an apology to justify them in making an immersionist Bible.

And, indeed, men who can make the charges they have made against the common version, prove that they are utterly incompetent to act in the capacity of critics. They are simply *mad* upon this subject; and no one need wonder if they should finally trample the holy oracles under their feet, like the Mormons and others; and, abandoning even the expedient of *translating*, to secure proof of their *peculiar dogma*, should seek for proof from some other source more likely to furnish it.

Their case reminds me of the advice of a Quaker to his son, when he first set out in the world to make a living. "Son," said he, "make money—*honestly*, if thee *can*—but *make money*." At all hazards they are determined to make capital for "*dip*, and *nothing but dip; immerse, and nothing but immerse*."

CHAPTER XI.

THE PORTION OF THE REVISION PUBLISHED.

In a former chapter I have referred to the portions of the new version that have been published and sent abroad. The only portions I have had an opportunity of seeing are the Second Epistle of Peter, and the Book of Revelation inclusive, and the first two chapters of Matthew.

The design of publishing these portions first in order is, doubtless, as I have already suggested, to avoid as long as possible coming before the world with their cherished idea of *dip* or *immerse* in the place of *baptize*. Consequently, they go no farther with Matthew than the second chapter. If they had embraced the third chapter of Matthew, or the First Epistle of Peter, the main design of the movement would have appeared at once. Immerse would have been "*printed—* PRINTED IN THE BIBLE," where they intend to have it ultimately. But they are anxious to keep off the evil day as long as they can. But we think it will be proper to call attention to what they have done in the work of translation, in order to see if they have acted upon the principles which they have so often announced as destined to govern them in the work.

1. The reader will recollect that one chief complaint against the common version is, that it is obscure on account of "*the Popish artifice* of transfer." That by this means the translators have "*wrapped up*" and concealed the true meaning of God's word "from the mass of the unlearned," "the common people," who constitute the majority. And the professed object of this movement was to "*take off the Popish covering from his pure word*," and "disabuse the public mind, led astray by doctors and dictionaries," etc.

The reader, no doubt, would think it strange indeed if it should appear after all that "*the*

Popish artifice" has been adopted by these ultra-honest men, who have had such a sympathy for *"the mass of the unlearned," " the common people."* I will take one specimen of the perspicuousness of this renowned new version, from the Book of Revelation, vi. 6. The common version reads thus:

"And I heard a voice in the midst of the four beasts say, A measure of wheat for a penny, and three measures of barley for a penny; and see thou hurt not the oil and the wine."

The new version has it:

"And I heard a voice in the midst of the four living creatures saying, A choenix of wheat for a denarius, and three choenixes of barley for a denarius."

There, now! is not that plain? "The common people," "the mass of the unlearned," know what *"denarius"* is! O yes! they can find out what it means by consulting Webster. And those of them who cannot afford to buy Webster, and cannot have access to it, must take for granted that the *faithful,* and honest, and learned translator knew, and that it is right, whether they know what it means or not! But "*choenix!*" "*choenix!*" what will they do with that? Could the unlearned always have access to Webster, he could not help them at all to a knowledge of its meaning. Webster is confined to a definition of terms already in use in the *English* language. But this "*choenix*" is an unnaturalized foreigner. Its meaning can only be known by reference to a Greek Lexicon. The word in the Greek is χοῖνιξ, "*choinix.*" All this *learned translator* has done is to substitute *e* in English for *iota* in Greek. Is this a *translation* or a *transfer?* Is this making the word of God *plain* to "*the common people?*"

How much more do the people know about "*denarius*" than "*penny,*" or about "*choenix*" than "*measure?*" And if the translators designed to make the thing so plain as to obviate the necessity of referring to commentaries or dictionaries, as they promised to do, why did they not substitute "*the eighth of a peck, or one quart,*" in the place of "*choenix,*" and "*seven *pence three farthings,* or *fourteen cents,*" in the place of "*denarius?*"

They have spoken of *baptize* as "a lizard crawling from a papal swamp." Well, what is "*choenix?*" It must be a *crocodile* or an *alligator.*

But let us have another specimen of perspicuity—of taking the Popish covering from God's pure word. It is found in Matthew ii. 1–7, 16. In all these verses, "*magians*" is put in the place of "*wise men.*"

Here we have another instance of "*the Popish artifice of transfer.*" The Greek is μάγοι, "*magoi.*" A slight variation of the original term is all that is done for the benefit of the illiterate "common people," the mass of the unlearned. This is *translation,* is it? Plain! perspicuous!

If some of the common people knew who these learned translators are, and where they live, they might write, or, if they should be too illiterate to do this, they might get one to write for them, and ask them to state what "*choenix,*" "*denarius,*" and "*magians*," mean. But "their names may not come abroad." It would "subject them to relentless persecution," and seriously annoy them in their great and learned work. So they must be content, and wait for the oracle at New York (the Board of Managers of the American Bible Union) to speak out again.

In a further notice of the new version that has appeared, I will call the attention of the reader to one of the rules which was to govern the translators in their work, and see if in the portion of it already done this rule has been observed. Here is the rule:

"2. The common English version must be made the basis of revision; and all unnecessary interference with the established phraseology shall be avoided; and only such alterations shall be made as the exact meaning of the inspired text and the existing state of the language may require."

I think it will appear that the translator of the two chapters of Matthew especially has not kept this rule. He discards the old and solemn style of the common version, by writing *appears*, instead of *appeareth*. In this he not only violates the above rule, and all good taste and judgment, but he disagrees with *the learned translator* of Peter, Jude, John's epistles, and the Revelation. He uniformly uses the termination TH, as *loveth, knoweth, hath, appeareth.*

This translator also discards *unto*, and seeks to impart a modern air to his work by substituting *to* in its stead. I quote a part of what he says to justify this literary *vandalism*. "The preposition '*unto*,' as found in the common version, is not used by good speakers and writers of the present day. Noah Webster says it is 'of no use in language: it is found in writers of former times, but is entirely obsolete.' In a thorough revision, therefore, this word, and all others that are in the same condition, must be rejected, unless the Book of God is to be kept throughout all ages as the repository of obsolete words and antiquated forms, and made to the common mind a *dead* letter, etc."

I refer as specimens of this change to Matthew 1. 20, etc. But the author of the revision of the epistles of Peter, John, Jude, and the Revelation, has retained "*unto*," and says in reference to it, "It would have been easy to impart a much more modern air to the whole by such expedients; for example, as exchanging *unto* for *to*, etc. But it is scarcely worth while to attempt an explanation of the reasons why the translator has refrained from doing this."

Now this revision will certainly be beautifully harmonious in its style! one portion retaining the "*unto*," and another rejecting it! And in what kind of a position do the American Bible Union stand? They have endorsed both these specimens, and sent them out. The translator of the specimen from Matthew says that "a thorough revision" requires the rejection of "*unto*," and thus condemns the translator of Peter, John, etc., who does not reject "*unto*," and thinks the reasons for not so doing are so clear that it is not necessary to name them. How will this thing be adjusted? The reader will recollect that the Board of Managers, through their Committee on Revision, have original jurisdiction of the whole matter, and of course they will determine it according to their own taste.

According to the principle adopted in rejecting *th* or *eth*, and *unto*, they should discard also *thou*, *thine*, *thy*, and *thee*. And, indeed, the translator of Matthew says: "In a thorough . . . . this word, ["*unto*,"] and all others that are in the same condition, must be rejected." Well, *thou*, *thine*, etc., are in the same condition, and, therefore, they ought to be rejected also; and then we should have: "Come TO me, all you that labor, and you shall find rest to your souls. Every one that LOVES, is born of God. Every one that ASKS, RECEIVES; and he that SEEKS, FINDS; whosoever HAS, to him shall be given." And when we pray we must say, according to modernizing doctrine, "Our Father, who are in heaven, hallowed be YOUR name : YOUR kingdom come, YOUR will be done . . . . for YOURS is the kingdom," etc.

Secretly is put for *privily*, Matthew i. 19. The common version reads : "Was minded to put her away privily." The new version: "Resolved to divorce her secretly."

In a note the translator says: "The common version does not correspond with the original. The Greek for 'privately' occurs elsewhere, but not here. The exact meaning of this adverb is 'secretly.'

But let any man look at Webster's Dictionary, and see if there is any ground for the distinction between the words *privily* and *secretly*, let the original word mean what it may. The question is as to which of these words ought to be used to express the meaning of the original.

Webster defines these words thus:

Privily, Privately; secretly.

Secretly, Privately; privily.

Privily, according to Webster, has as many rights as *secretly* to have the place it occupies in the common version. And, therefore, if it is not a translation of the original, neither is *secretly*.

In Matthew ii. 16, "angry" is put in the place of "wroth."

In his note the translator says: "The adjective 'wroth' is falling into disuse among good speakers and writers of the English language, and is not, therefore, the best term for a correct translation."

But what does Webster say? "*Wroth*, very angry; much exasperated. An excellent word, and not obsolete."

I quote the following from the New York Observer, as referring to a portion of the new version which I have not seen:

"The first time that the new version of the Bible has been brought into the pulpit to use, was at the funeral-services of the late Rev. Dr. Cone. As he was one of its fathers, it was meet that his obsequies should be signalized by the inauguration of his favorite work. The Rev. Dr. McClay read selections from the book of Job, according to the new version, in the midst of which occurred the following passage: 'And Satan went out from the presence of Jehovah, and smote Job with grievous ulcers, from the sole of his foot to his crown. And he took a potsherd to scrape himself therewith, as he ⎰ among the ashes. Then said his wife to hi ⎱ Dost thou still hold fast thy integrity? Bl God and die! But Job said to her, Thou spe: est as one of the foolish women speaks. ℩ good shall we receive from God, and shall we not receive the evil?'

"If these astute and professedly learned critics have found any sufficient reason for substituting 'grievous ulcers' for 'sore boils,' we will not quarrel with them for the liberty they have taken. Sore boils are grievous ulcers, if not *vice versâ*, and we are always glad to let them pass. The least said the better about boils. But not so the new phase they give to the language and sentiment of Job's wife.

"Our translation reads: 'Then said his wife unto him, Dost thou still retain thine integrity? Curse God and die.' The new translators render it, 'Bless God and die.' Is there any thing to favor this change? We are aware that modern critics (as Dr. Mason Goode) have given it: 'Dost thou still retain thine integrity, *blessing*

God and *dying?*' And this reading preserves the wife's idea, for she complains of Job for still trusting in God even in his extremity. And then we see the force of his reply: 'Thou speakest as one of the foolish women speaketh. What! shall we receive good at the hand of God, and shall we not receive evil?'

"But if we make Job's wife to advise her husband to BLESS God and die, as there was every reason to suppose he was about to die, his reply to her is inhuman and wicked; and it could not be affirmed of him, as it is affirmed, 'In all this did not Job sin with his lips.'

"'The response of Job,' says Barnes, 'shows that he understood her as exciting him to reject, renounce, or curse God. The sense is, that she regarded him as unworthy of confidence.'

"It requires no great knowledge of the ancient Scriptures to expose the glaring absurdity and positive wrong of this Baptist version's alteration of God's holy word.

"We know that the word rendered *curse* may also be translated *bless*, as its more precise meaning is to invoke, *i. e.*, either good or evil, to be determined by the context. The same word in the Hebrew is used in 1 Kings xxi. 10-13, where the sons of Belial are hardly to be suspected of charging Naboth with *blessing* God and the king. In the case of Job and his wife, the whole conversation proceeds on the presumption that *she* exhorts the patient and submissive patriarch to *curse* God, and not *bless* him, as he had done (chapter i. 21) with all the fervor of his soul, in words that are even to this day the language only of a heart perfectly resigned to God's will. Such, too, has been the uniform sentiment of the Church in all ages and climes. Job's wife has been remembered for her wicked assault upon her husband in this calamity, as truly as Lot's wife for looking back when she and her husband were fleeing from Sodom. We have called attention to this obvious alteration of the sacred text, to expose not only the incompetency, but the recklessness of these new version tinkers.

"If they will thus mar the beauty and destroy the meaning of God's word in portions of the

Holy Scriptures where there is no difference of opinion among Christians, what will they not do when the powerful motive of sectarian prejudice urges them to tamper with the sacred text?

"It is evident that they have no claim whatever to consideration on the score of learning or ability; and we predict that their new Bible will react upon the cause they are hoping to serve by getting it up."

I might add many authorities to justify the common version of Job ii. 9, such as Orton, Henry, Scott, etc. But I will content myself with giving a quotation from the late Dr. John Kitto, of England, one of the most profoundly learned biblical critics and scholars of this or any other age. I am more inclined to give his authority, as the advocates of the new version movement put so much stress upon the progress of biblical criticism since our common version was made, as a reason for a new one. Well, Dr. Kitto is as modern a critic as can be desired, and one thoroughly versed in biblical learning.

I quote from his "Daily Bible Illustrations" of the Book of Job, p. 93 :

"Therefore, when she saw that her husband's faith was not shaken even by this sore distress, she cried, 'Dost thou still retain thine integrity? Curse God and die.' Surely words so dreadful never before nor since came from a woman's lips."

Again he says: "Job's answer to this suggestion—in which we fail not to trace Satan's hand—is worthy of his faith and patience: 'Thou speakest as one of the foolish women speaketh. What! shall we receive good at the hand of the Lord, and not evil?'"

Again, on p. 95, after giving various opinions in regard to the import of the words of Job's wife under consideration, he refers to the view of their meaning adopted by the translator of the Book of Job for the American Bible Union, as follows: "There is, however, another explanation, which, acknowledging the force of this consideration, gives a bad sense to the advice of Job's wife, while retaining the sense of *bless-*

ing instead of *cursing* God. This is accomplished by making her words ironical, as if she had said, 'Ay, do go on still, relying upon thine integrity, and blessing God, and yet dying; for he will not save thee.' But surely of all things irony would be most misplaced here. Consider that she herself was a most afflicted woman, and that the wickedness of rebellious thoughts and language under extreme sorrow is far more natural than irony.

"There are other explanations of the words, both as taken in the sense of 'bless' and 'curse;' but the reader has had a sufficient variety. Upon the whole, the interpretation we have given seems best to meet all the circumstances."

CHAPTER XII.

CONCLUSION.

In this chapter I will present a synopsis of the leading arguments, and some little additional matter upon a few points.

The reader will bear in mind the real issue involved in the discussion—not that there are errors in the commonly received version; nor that there ought to be a new version; but this is the question: whether there ought to be such a version as the American Bible Union is seeking, i. e., a strictly *sectarian* one—*immerse and its cognates* being substituted for *baptize and its cognates*. *This is the question.*

As the advocates of the movement try to deny that such is intended to be the character of their version, I have been constrained, for the present, to decline the discussion of the *main question* upon its merits, and to proceed to prove that the *design*, and the *main design*, is the substitution of immerse for baptize.

I. This I have satisfactorily done—1. From the history of the movement in India, in this country, and in Great Britain. We have seen that Dr. Judson and four others consulted Professor Stuart as to whether they should transfer *baptizo*, or translate it by words signifying *immerse*. And notwithstanding Professor Stuart advised them to transfer, as had been done in the Latin, French, and English, yet Dr. Judson proceeded to make his Burmese version upon immersionist principles.

In the meantime, other Baptist missionaries, Pearce and Yates, were making the same kind of a version into the Bengalee tongue; and learning that this was the character of it, the Calcutta Bible Society refused any longer to patronize it. The British and Foreign Bible Society had assumed the same ground in reference to such versions. Not being able to secure aid from any other society, and learning that the American Bible Society were aiding Dr. Judson's version, which they knew to be of the same character with their own, they wrote to the Society requesting aid. The Society learning in this way, for the first time, the character of Judson's version, not only refused to grant aid to Pearce and Yates, but withdrew their support from Judson's.

They were constrained to do this in accordance with the very principles upon which the Society was originally organized. And I have most satisfactorily shown, from the best authority, that there is no just ground of complaint against the Society.

I have shown that, in India, Great Britain, and in this country, the Baptists seceded from the Bible societies in these three quarters of the globe, because those societies would not appropriate money, contributed by all denominations, to aid in publishing *sectarian* versions of the narrowest kind.

And why was the Baptist Bible Society (the "American and Foreign") formed? Simply on account of the devotion of the Baptists to *immersion*. Why was the British Translation Society organized under the auspices of the American and Foreign Bible Society, through their agent, Dr. McClay? Why, in order to secure immersionist versions of the Scriptures, as is demonstrated by one article of their constitution, which requires that, in all translations they will patronize, the words relating to the ordinance of baptism must be translated by words signifying immerse.

And finally, why, in 1850, did Dr. Cone and others secede from the American and Foreign Bible Society, and form the American Bible Union? Why, simply and exclusively because the American and Foreign Bible Society decided, by an overwhelming majority, to recede from the purpose they at one time entertained, of carrying out the same principle in reference to the English Scriptures which they had been from the beginning carrying out in reference to all their translations into foreign tongues, and which they are still maintaining: that is, to have an English translation of the Holy Scriptures on *immersionist* principles. To secure such a version is the leading and controlling purpose of the American Bible Union. This is the thing which distinguishes this institution from the American and Foreign Bible Society.

2. I have adduced quotations from the reports of the American and Foreign Bible Society, the Bible Translation Society of Great Britain, and of the American Bible Union, and also from the speeches and addresses and other publications of the leading advocates of the new version movement, in this country, Asia and Europe, in which there is sore complaint against the Bible societies of Europe, Asia, and America, for not giving the heathen *immerse* as the translation of *baptizo*, in the versions into foreign languages, and in the English language—that thus the heathen are "left to perish in their ignorance and idolatry," without having a knowledge of baptism—that in the common version in English the ordinance "*is covered up and hid*" from the mass of the people by "THE POPISH ARTIFICE OF TRANSFER"—that "*it is wrapped up in obscurity*," and can only be known by "*the learned*"—that

the great principle "*to vindicate*" which the American and Foreign Bible Society was organized is, that in translations into all languages, "*baptizo and its cognates should be rendered by words signifying immerse, immersion,*" etc.; and that this Society receding from the great purpose of its original organization, as far as the English Scriptures are concerned, the American Bible Union assumes its place, and proposes to accomplish this "great work"—that the aim of the Union is to have "*immerse printed*—PRINTED IN THE BIBLE."

I have quoted from the speeches of several distinguished advocates of the movement, in which the admission is distinctly and unequivocally made, that the English word *baptize* is a word of *generic* import, having lost what they contend was its *specific* import, to *immerse*, which they say it had in the days of Elizabeth, and when our translation was made; and they propose, as *baptize* has become *a lying old sinner*, to turn it out of the Bible, and out of the Church, and bring in immerse into its place.

3. Having thus adduced in part what the leaders in this enterprise have *said*, as to the *main design*, I have proceeded to show what they have actually *done*, as settling the question beyond the possibility of cavil.

I have quoted from the edition of the New Testament published by the American and Foreign Bible Society, with the meaning of *baptize* and *baptism* given on "a fly-leaf," in a glossary, as *immerse* and *immersion*.

I have also quoted from the edition of Cone and Wyckoff, with *immerse, immersion*, and their cognates, incorporated into the text in the place of *baptize, baptism*, etc.

These editions were published by the American and Foreign Bible Society long before they gave up their purpose of having an immersionist version of the English Scriptures, and they were sent out among the Baptists in order to prepare them for that which was to follow in due course.

I have presented a specimen of the translation into the Siamese tongue, in which *baptizo*, etc., are translated by words signifying *immerse, immer-*

IMMERSIONISTS AGAINST THE BIBLE. 253

sion, etc. And the editor of the Bible Union Reporter approves of this translation, as in accordance with the great principle governing the movement.

I have referred to the *Spanish* and *Italian* versions. I will here give a specimen from the former, as published in the Bible Union Reporter for October, 1853. Here it is in the Spanish language:

"MATEO, CAP. III.

"11. Yo, si, *sumerjo* en agua en [profesion de] arrepentimiento; pero el que viene en pos de mí, mas fuerte es que yo, cuyo calzado no soi digno de lleverale: él os sumergirá en Espíritu Santo, i en fuego."

Now, here, as the reader will observe, the word "*sumerjo,*" in Spanish, is given as the rendering of *baptizo*. And this word, indicating by its very form its origin from the Latin, means nothing but *immerse* or *plunge*. I repeat again, we have in these translations what the Union have actually *done,* as demonstrating what kind of a version we are to expect in English.

It is true, as I have shown, they in so many

words deny that the design is to substitute *immerse* for *baptize*, and adduce the rules as merely requiring that the original be "*faithfully translated.*" But we know very well what they mean by "faithful translations." They are such as, at least, have *immerse* in the place of *baptize*, and this can be secured without violating the rules, as I have shown. And that it can be done in accordance with the rules in the estimation of the Union *itself*, is positively demonstrated by the fact that they have had such versions made, and have approved of them as in accordance with the great principle governing the Union in the work of translation; and they have published them and sent them abroad as "*specimens.*"

II. I have next noticed some of the *dishonorable*, and, as I think, *unchristian*, expedients which are adopted to *hoodwink* the public as to the *main design* of the movement. I will here recur to the principal of these expedients, before noticed, as showing up the kind of *tactics* adopted to carry forward what its advocates style " the greatest enterprise of the age."

1. I have noticed the effort to make a false impression upon the public mind by representing that all the denominations of Protestant Christians are engaged in it—both in Europe and America. And I see in a late number of the "Western Recorder," published at Louisville, Ky., that they are claiming the Roman Catholics as in favor of it. They might just as well go on and say that the whole world, ecclesiastical, political, and literary, are in favor of it—Jews, Mohammedans, and Heathens. Having loosed their moorings from the haven of honesty and candor, they might as well keep out at sea, and say any thing at all that will serve their purpose.

I have shown that the Pedobaptists engaged in this enterprise, either as members of the Union or as translators, are not in any sense the representatives of the Churches to which they belong. If they are, where and when were they appointed as such, and where is the record of it? And if the Pedobaptist Churches are represented, why do none of them appear as officers of the

Union? Why do not some of them appear as its advocates at their anniversaries? Why do no Pedobaptist journals advocate the great principle of the Union? Why are none of the Pedobaptists employed as agents to travel through the country and advocate revision? Let these questions be answered before this statement is made any more.

As to the Pedobaptists engaged as translators, (and they say a majority of their translators are of this class,) they admit in their own publications that they are employed "*under written contract.*" They are only doing *a literary job* for the Union. They have sold themselves to the Bible Union for the time, for " *a mess of pottage,*" which, I have no doubt, the poor fellows needed very much.

But it matters not who are the translators. Their work has to be scanned by the committee on versions of the Bible Union before it can see the light. This committee, and another, called an "*ultimate committee,*" must be pleased with its merits in all respects. And of whom are these committees composed? Why, *immersionists*, and none but *immersionists*.

2. Another feature in the tactics of this "*greatest enterprise*," is the publication of certain portions of the new version, which do not contain the real issue; and they have sent these abroad as "*specimens*" of the forthcoming completed version. The portions, as the reader will recollect I have stated, do not contain *baptizo*, nor any of its derivatives, in the original; and, therefore, the translators could not come out with the main design in these portions. Why did they not, I have inquired, publish the third chapter of Matthew and the second epistle of Peter? Why, simply, because this would have opened the eyes of the public to the main design, which they aim to avoid. They have, by this unfair course, had these "*specimens*" *puffed*, and have published the commendations of a large number of learned men in England and America as favorable to the enterprise as such.

I will here, however, present one "*specimen*"

of the manner, doubtless, in which many, if not all, of these commendations have been secured.

I quote from the New York Observer for January 3, 1856, as follows: "The use which has been made of the names of gentlemen in other Christian denominations, to give currency to the new version, is, in our view, worthy of specific censure, inasmuch as it lacks that Christian fairness and candor which should peculiarly characterize the movement of all religious associations. As an example of the use which has been made of distinguished names, we copy the following correspondence between the Rev. E. B. Raffensperger and Dr. J. A. Alexander:

"BELLEFONTAINE, O., Nov. 27, 1855.

"DEAR SIR:—To-day I dined with one of the families of my Church, in company with a certain Baptist minister, who is in the employ of the 'Bible Union.' He stated, in the presence of the company, that you had given your '*unqualified approval* of the operations of that Society.' In reply to my question, he also stated that he is in the habit of using the influence of your name from the pulpit on the Sabbath, while urging the claims of the 'Bible Union.' Will you be kind enough to state whether this man has really any authority for making such use of the venerated name of one of my Princeton instructors?

"Yours, respectfully,
"E. B. RAFFENSPERGER.
"REV. J. A. ALEXANDER, D.D."

"PRINCETON, N. J., Dec. 5, 1855.

"MY DEAR SIR :—I have again and again contradicted the absurd and false report that I approve of the new Baptist Bible. It has grown out of a friendly expression of opinion as to the literary merit of that part of the revision executed by a minister of our own Church, the Rev. John Lillie, of New York. That opinion has no more to do with the question of a new version to replace the common one, than my own translation of Isaiah and the Psalms, which I would not, if I could, put into the place of the authorized version. While I look upon new translations as an important part of interpretation, I think the scheme of a new Bible to replace the old one as inexpedient and impracticable in itself, as the use of my name by its advocates, after my repeated public contradiction, is *dishonest and unchristian*. For confirmation of these statements, I refer to the Rev. John Lillie, at the office of the 'Bible Union' itself.

"Yours, very truly,
"J. A. ALEXANDER.
"REV. E. B. RAFFENSPERGER."

And in the Observer of the 17th of the same month there is published the following from the Rev. Mr. Lillie, to whom Dr. Alexander refers in the above letter.

"AMERICAN BIBLE UNION ROOMS, Jan. 8, 1856.

"MESSRS. EDITORS:—In your last number I observed a letter from the Rev. Dr. J. A. Alexander, of Princeton, in which, after briefly explaining what it was that has led some, it would appear, to represent him as favorable to an enterprise of which he disapproves, to wit, that of the American Bible Union, he refers his correspondent for fuller information to myself. Let this be my apology for troubling you with the following statement.

"Some three years ago I printed a work of mine on the Second Epistle of Peter, and the Epistles of John and Jude. And it was in relation to this that I received from Dr. Alexander, toward the close of 1852, a written expression of his opinion. In the summer of 1854, the same work was reprinted, in greatly enlarged form, and with the addition of the Book of Revelation, the whole making a volume of five times the size of its predecessor. When, therefore, I returned from Europe in the fall of the year last mentioned, and, on the day of my landing, found in the printed abstract of the Annual Report, prepared for the annual meeting of the Society then in session, a few commendatory words extracted from that private letter, and which now also might be taken as an endorsement of the latter publication, I was, indeed, not a little chagrined. It was nearly two years since I had consented that a communication, in which the brethren of the Bible Union naturally felt themselves interested, should be copied at their rooms, but with an express understanding, as I did most assuredly suppose, that nothing of it whatever should be published without the writer's consent first asked and obtained: though it must be confessed, on the other hand, that, in my inquiries on the subject, the Secretary disclaims all recollection of any such restriction. However, I wrote immediately to Dr. Alexander, expressing my deep regret at what had occurred, and offering to make whatever public amends was still in my power. In very kind terms he relieved me of that necessity; and the Secretary himself then proposed, as I also informed Dr. Alexander, that in the Annual Report, which had not yet appeared, the reference of the extract to the first specimen of revision should be distinctly defined, or, if Dr. Alexander preferred, the extract should be suppressed altogether. The former alternative was the one finally adopted.

"I am, etc.,

"JOHN LILLIE."

Now, I would ask, in view of the light afforded in the above correspondence as to the manner in which Dr. Alexander's commendation of the new version was secured, what confidence can be reposed in the legitimacy of any of the numerous commendations they have published, and which are read and commented on by the agents of the Union throughout the length and breadth of the land, in order, if possible, *to swindle* the people out of their money?

Who knows but that the whole of them have been secured in the same *fraudulent* and *dishonest* way?

3. I have referred to the manner in which King James and the translators of the common version, and the version itself, have been abused by the friends of this movement, as a means of making way for their own *one-sided, sectarian* production. But I have proved from the highest authority, and *Baptist* authority at that, 1. That James was not legally acknowledged as king of England at the time the translation was determined upon. 2. That the motion for a new translation did not

originate with James, nor the Episcopal party, but was made by Dr. Rainolds, *a Puritan*, or *Presbyterian*. 3. That James did not select the translators: he only approved of the selection made. 4. That neither James nor the government of England ever recognized the enterprise, or ever paid one penny to defray the expenses of it. 5. That the common version did not gain the ascendency over other versions then and for many years after published, as the result of any interference of royal or governmental authority, but as the result of its own intrinsic merits.

As to the rules prescribed for the direction of the translators, of which there has been so much complaint, as *fettering* them, I have shown, 1. That the rules do not prohibit translation from the original at all, in any sense. 2. That the word baptize is not once named in the rules as one of the words to be retained. 3. That the only absolute restriction which the rules lay upon the translators is, that they shall be faithful to the original Hebrew and Greek. 4. That the translators certainly did not understand the rules as prohibiting the translation of *baptizo;* for they have positively translated it, at least in three instances: one in Heb. ix. 10, and twice in Mark vii. 4.

But I have proved that the very thing which they have charged King James with doing, without the slightest foundation, the American Bible Union have done themselves. *They have left to their translators no independent discretion at all.* In addition to what I have adduced from their own publications to demonstrate this *astounding fact,* I will furnish the reader with an additional quotation from the Semi-annual Report of the American Bible Union for 1855, as published in the Bible Union Reporter for June, 1855, which lies before me. Listen to what the Board of Managers say:

"When a scholar is engaged by the Board, instructions are introduced into the contract, requiring the exact meaning of the original; and he is requested and urged to make the most thorough and faithful version possible. No expense is spared to furnish him with needed books, and other requisite facilities. *When his work is finished, the manuscript is submitted to the Board, and referred to the committee on versions. This committee is required to give it a careful examination, and not to recommend its printing unless its merits will justify such an expenditure. If this is not the case, another scholar or other scholars are employed on the same part. Sometimes the work has to go through the hands of a third or fourth party before the committee feel justified in printing it. On some parts we have manuscripts from five different hands. All of these are of more or less service in the prosecution of the work; and ultimately will greatly aid the ultimate committee that must prepare the whole book for the press."*

Did King James or any other *despot* ever institute such a system of *surveillance* over a set of translators before?

And in view of the account above given by the Union itself, what independent discretion, I ask again, do these notable and "*learned*" translators enjoy?

4. Another expedient which I have noticed, is the representation that other denominations have had their denominational translations, and that, consequently, there should be no complaint of the immersionists for having one. If they had appealed to the example of the Papists, the Swedenborgians, the Universalists, the Unitarians, and the sect of the Destructionists, to justify their measure, there would have been some appropriateness in it. For all these have versions, or rather *perversions* of the Holy Scriptures conforming to their faith and usages.

But where is any sectarianism, for instance, in Wesley's translation of the New Testament? Where is there any in Doddridge's or Macknight's, unless it be in opposition to the prevailing opinion and practice of their own sect in regard to baptism? And again: Did any of these learned men intimate that his version was designed to supersede the common version? Or have any of these denominations intimated a desire that such should be the case? or has any such thing been attempted?

Conybeare has been quoted as favorable to this

movement, because he has given, in his late translation of Paul's epistles, variations from the common version, though, perhaps, he never heard of the Bible Union. But we have quoted the language of him and Mr. Howson speaking of the common version as "unrivalled."

The same claim is made in reference to every learned man who has taken any exceptions to the manner in which any passage in the common version is translated. All he says is construed and published as so much said in favor of this movement, though he may have expressed in the most unequivocal manner his admiration of the common version as a whole. This remark applies to Dr. Adam Clarke, and many others.

Nothing these men have said can be legitimately construed in favor of this movement, unless it can be shown that they have expressed themselves in favor of the *main design*—that is, the substitution of *immerse* for baptize in the common version. Have they done this?

As to what the American Bible Society have recently done, I have shown that they have made no translation at all, but merely a "*collation*," for the purpose, *mainly*, of restoring our copy of the Bible to the edition of 1611. They have made some correction of errors in orthography, punctuation, capital letters, etc.

And then, again, we have asked, even if the American Bible Society have made a translation, (and they have not,) is there any change which they have made favorable to the doctrines or practice of any sect, or any class of sects?

III. I have briefly examined some of the changes proposed in the common version, and have shown, I think, very conclusively, that none of them are demanded by fidelity to the original, while many of them are an outrage upon good taste and sound biblical criticism.

IV. I have finally offered a brief criticism on the portions of the new version that I have been able to secure, and have shown that whatever may be the merit of some of the changes they have made, they have violated their own principles of translation, so loudly and repeatedly announced, and have done violence to the rules of good taste and sound scholarship.

And I think the reflecting among the devotees of this movement will be constrained, after a while, to feel the force of the prophet's language, if the "*specimens*" already published indicate the character of their version : "Hath a nation changed their gods, which are yet no gods? But my people have changed their glory for that which doth not profit?"

Many a good, pious Baptist, (and there are such,) if this new version should prevail, will feel like Mary did when she said, "They have taken away my Lord, and I know not where they have laid him." No person deeply imbued with piety, not to say sound learning or good judgment, can ever finally give up "The Old-fashioned Bible" for any such a *mutilated and spiritless thing*, apart from its *narrow sectarian* character. "No man, having drunk old wine, straightway desireth new; for he saith the old is better."

THE END.

www.ingramcontent.com/pod-product-compliance
Lightning Source LLC
Chambersburg PA
CBHW031252250426
43672CB00029BA/2180